JOBS AND INCOMES IN A GLOBALIZING WORLD

JOBS AND INCOMES IN A GLOBALIZING WORLD

AJIT K. GHOSE

INTERNATIONAL LABOUR OFFICE • GENEVA

Ghose, A.K.
Jobs and incomes in a globalizing world
Geneva, International Labour Office, 2003

Employment, wages, globalization of the economy, trend, developed country, developing country. 13.01.3

ISBN 92-2-112717-6

ILO Cataloguing in Publication Data

ILO publications can be obtained through major booksellers or ILO local offices in many countries, or direct from ILO Publications, International Labour Office, CH-1211 Geneva 22, Switzerland. Catalogues or lists of new publications are available free of charge from the above address or by email: pubvente@ilo.org.

Typeset by Magheross Graphics, France & Ireland *www.magheross.com*
Printed and bound in Great Britain by Biddles Ltd. www.biddles.co.uk

CONTENTS

Tables

Figures

ACKNOWLEDGEMENTS

My greatest debts are to my research collaborators – Bishwanath Goldar, Michael Landesmann, Sandra Leitner, Gabriel Palma, Rajah Rasiah, Ruoen Ren, Robert Stehrer, Matias Vernengo and Wing Thye Woo – without whose inputs I could not have written this book; to Makiko Matsumoto who helped me in many different ways; to Albi Tola who provided very helpful research assistance; and to Christine Alfthan who carried the burden of producing a clean manuscript with a smile. Dharam Ghai and Samir Radwan read through the entire manuscript and provided helpful comments. I benefited from discussions with fellow researchers in and outside the ILO: Manolo Abella, Rolph van der Hoeven, Eivind Hoffmann, David Kucera, Sanjaya Lall, Eddy Lee, Nomaan Majid, Ferhad Mehran, Peter Peek, Ashwani Saith and Adrian Wood. Rosemary Beattie saved me from quite a few stylistic errors, and Charlotte Beauchamp did a deft editing of the manuscript. Active encouragement from several colleagues – Rashid Amjad, Peter Auer, Duncan Campbell, David Freedman, Göran Hultin and Mohammed Muqtada – kept my spirits up. To all of them, my sincere thanks.

INTRODUCTION 1

This book addresses a specific question: What have been the effects of globalization, as it has progressed so far, on jobs, wages and incomes in industrialized and developing countries? The question has dominated both public discussions and academic debates, but it has most often been asked with reference to the industrialized countries alone. Yet globalization is about the economic integration of industrialized and developing countries. Its effects in the two types of countries are closely interrelated and must be viewed together for a proper assessment of the costs and benefits. This proposition constitutes a basic premise for the book.

The nature of the question itself should indicate to the reader what the book does not deal with. In the first place, it takes the process of globalization as a given. This means that the flaws in the process, which are many, are not examined in any detail or depth. A number of recent studies provide fairly detailed analysis of the flaws – the biases in the trade rules, the inappropriateness of the rules relating to intellectual property rights, the new forms of non-tariff trade barriers, and the grave limitations of the global institutions of governance arising from their undemocratic character.[1] This book focuses not on these flaws but on certain outcomes of the flawed process of globalization: those relating to employment and incomes. There are widespread popular concerns and anxieties about globalization, which centre largely on the perceived uncertainties relating to these outcomes. A serious scrutiny of the facts and the arguments is required to know if these concerns and anxieties are well founded. And such a scrutiny must also be deemed necessary if we are to form proper judgements on the flaws of the process of globalization and on possible ways of rectifying them.

[1] See, for example, Oxfam (2002) and Stiglitz (2002).

Second, the analysis focuses only on industrialized and developing countries, and leaves out the European transition countries in particular. One reason is that most of the current issues and concerns actually relate to trade between North (the industrialized countries) and South (the developing countries). While the Asian transition countries can more easily be identified as developing countries, it is hard to decide how to categorize European transition countries. The other reason is analytical. The observed developments in the European transition countries arise from complex interactions between two simultaneous processes: the systemic transition from a centrally planned to a market economy and the process of globalization. For this reason, it is difficult to analyse the developments in these countries within a framework that is deemed appropriate for analysing the developments in industrialized and developing countries, developments that are linked more clearly to globalization. In view of these considerations, the only transition country included in the analysis of the core issues in the book is China, which can legitimately be treated as a developing country where systemic transition preceded globalization.

Third, globalization, it is well known, has increased the frequency of economic crisis around the world. The 1990s alone witnessed the Mexican crisis, the East Asian crisis, the Russian crisis and the Brazilian crisis. These crises have had sharply adverse short-run effects on employment and wages in the affected countries,[2] and there is widespread agreement that finding ways of preventing the recurrence of such crises in future is an urgent task facing the international community.[3] In this book, however, we do not attempt to analyse these short-run effects; we abstract from them in order to focus on the more general medium-term trends.

The point of departure for the book is a particular view of the process of globalization. This view, derived from an empirical identification of the central characteristics of globalization, can be briefly stated as follows.

There is little reason to doubt that freer trade has been the main driving force for the process of globalization. Freer capital flow has had an important but essentially supportive role to play. And labour flow, which is no freer today than it was two decades ago, has naturally had no role. But, though trade has been the driving force for globalization, the core of the process is not mere growth of trade. The core is the growth of two-way trade in manufactures

[2] See, for example, Lee (1998).

[3] The crises have been extensively analysed, and there is now a consensus that they are attributable basically to premature liberalization of national financial markets. International financial markets are highly imperfect and lack an appropriate regulatory framework. In this setting, liberalization of inadequately developed national financial markets carries grave risks. Thus, if crises are to be prevented, extreme caution must be exercised in opening up financial markets of developing countries, and an appropriate regulatory framework for international financial markets must be put in place. See IMF (2001), UNCTAD (1998) and Stiglitz (2002).

between North and South, which implies a fairly fundamental restructuring of the long-established international division of labour. One side of this restructuring is the emergence of a number of low-income developing countries as major exporters of manufactures. The other side is global exclusion or "marginalization" of those developing countries that lacked the capacity to develop manufactures and, consequently, have remained overwhelmingly dependent on exports of primary commodities.

Given this view of globalization, two presumptions follow. First, it does not require much research to say that the outcomes of globalization for employment and incomes in the globally excluded developing countries have been unfavourable. But this has to do with exclusion rather than with integration (and the associated restructuring of the international division of labour). The real issue in this context is how to overcome exclusion. If our objective is to understand the effects of integration on employment and incomes, therefore, we need to focus not on these excluded countries but on countries that are actually integrating themselves into the global economy. This is why we focus on the industrialized countries on the one hand and a selected set of developing countries (the developing countries that have emerged as important exporters of manufactures) on the other.

Second, because the growth of North–South manufactured trade constitutes the core of globalization, its primary effects are on employment and wages in manufacturing industries. In studying these effects, therefore, we can legitimately confine attention to these industries alone. The economy-wide effects, which we only touch upon in this book, depend on the role and the importance of manufacturing industries in the particular economy in question. In general, the economy-wide effects would be much less significant in industrialized countries, where services account for the bulk of employment and the transfer of labour from manufacturing into services is a sign of dynamism, than in developing countries, where economic transformation requires labour transfer from agriculture and other traditional activities into manufacturing.

While an assessment of the effects of globalization on employment and wages in the manufacturing industries of the integrating countries is our major concern in this volume, we have thought it appropriate to analyse a few related issues of global concern. The first is the issue of global income inequality and the way this has been affected by globalization. An investigation into this issue can be seen as a probe into the phenomena of inclusion and exclusion. But it also provides a broad view of the way globalization has affected economic growth and incomes across the world. The second issue is that of international migration. This, as noted above, has been the missing element of globalization so far; there are no obvious signs of a global labour market emerging.

Nevertheless, there are good reasons to view it as an emerging area of concern. Globalization is likely to change the pattern, if not the extent, of international migration. And the pattern of international migration affects national labour markets and also has consequences for trade and growth. The final issue concerns the linkage between trade and labour standards. If trade affects employment and wages, it can be expected to affect labour standards too, and there is widespread concern that the effects are adverse. At the same time, if trade and labour standards are linked, then trade could arguably be regarded as a potential instrument for improving labour standards in countries where they are inappropriately low.

The book is based on original empirical research, carried out at the International Labour Office (ILO), and on a thorough review of the available literature. A combination of cross-country analysis and case studies has been employed in the empirical research. In analysing the effects of North–South trade on employment and wages in manufacturing, detailed case studies have been relied upon. Given the limitations of time and resources, only a limited number of such case studies could be carried out. But the selection of cases for study was based on preliminary investigations and much thought so that the results could be generalized with a fair degree of confidence. In studying issues of global concern, such as those of global income inequality and international migration, the method of cross-country analysis was employed.

The plan of the book is as follows. In Chapter 2, we examine the specific developments that define globalization. This generates the basic premise for the analysis in the rest of the book: the growth of two-way trade in manufactures between the industrialized countries and a select group of developing countries constitutes the core of the process of globalization. It is this development that has given rise to the issues analysed in the subsequent chapters. In Chapter 3, the recent trends in global income inequality are analysed. The extent to which globalization, or more specifically trade, may have contributed to these trends is also studied. In Chapter 4, the core chapter of the book, the effects of trade on manufacturing employment and wages in a set of sample countries – consisting of both industrialized and developing countries – are analysed. Chapter 5 examines the facts about international migration. It also considers how the pattern of international migration might be affected by globalization and the problems that such changes might generate. In Chapter 6, we draw on the findings of the preceding chapters to consider if there are reasons to believe that globalization threatens to undermine labour standards worldwide. We also examine the extent to which trade can serve as an instrument for promoting labour standards in low-income developing countries. The concluding chapter outlines the important policy issues that emerge from the analysis presented in the book.

GLOBALIZATION: CHARACTERISTICS, ISSUES AND CONCERNS 2

What is globalization?

Globalization is a widely used term, but one that still lacks a clear definition. It conveys different meanings to different people, and there are good reasons why this is so. Globalization is a complex and multidimensional process; it is natural that it should present different faces to different individuals, groups and nations. For analytical purposes, however, we need a clearly defined term. We need to start by stating what we mean by globalization. Our purpose is not to enter into a debate about what the true meaning of globalization is or should be (though a debate is perhaps desirable), but simply to alert the reader to the particular meaning that we attach to the term in this book.

Globalization is a process of integration of national markets into a global market. Markets, of course, exist not only in products but also in what economists call factors of production – essentially capital and labour (but one could add skills). Globalization then is the process of formation of global markets in products as well as in factors of production. This definition immediately calls attention to the fact that globalization must be a process stretched over a long time horizon. Many countries do not as yet have integrated national markets and it is difficult to envisage the emergence of truly global markets in the foreseeable future. Recognition of this prompts us to ask the following question. If integration is only partial and is likely to remain so in the foreseeable future, what is particularly new about globalization today? Supra-national markets, after all, started emerging centuries ago and even the least developed country has a long history of participation in such markets. An earlier period of globalization (1870–1913) is much discussed today. The post-war integration of the advanced industrialized nations pre-dates the current globalization period as it is normally defined; the period 1950–73, which is referred to as the "golden age", could also be characterized as the second wave of globalization (although there were important restrictions on the mobility of labour and capital, the period witnessed both the rapid growth of manufactured trade among industrialized countries and the development of international institutions of governance). Why, then, should we be so preoccupied with globalization now?

The reason is that some important new forces have come into play since the mid-1980s – the years generally regarded as the beginning of the current process of globalization. First, there have been fairly important improvements in transportation and communication technologies, leading to a significant decline in costs. Apart from facilitating trade in general, the growing ease and declining costs of freight, travel and communication have the potential for restructuring the international division of labour. For they make it both possible and profitable to split production processes into component parts that could be undertaken in multiple units scattered across the world. As such, they have created (or at least substantially enhanced) the possibility of a new kind of trade in intermediate manufactured products, i.e., products that are destined not for final consumption but for use as inputs in the manufacture of other products.[1] All this is reflected in the growing importance of transnational corporations (TNCs) in global production and exports.[2] Rough estimates show that, between 1982 and 1999, foreign affiliates of TNCs increased their share of world gross domestic product (GDP) from 5 per cent to 10 per cent and their share of world exports from 31 per cent to 45 per cent. Employment in these enterprises in 1999 was 2.3 times that in 1982.[3]

Second, import-substitution industrialization strategies have gone out of existence as virtually all countries in the developing world have implemented trade liberalization policies. This has resulted in universal reduction of tariff rates and non-tariff trade barriers, particularly since the mid-1980s.[4] It is true that some countries implemented trade liberalization policies under compulsion, as this constituted a condition for assistance from the Bretton Woods institutions, but others freely chose to adopt them. Industrialization strategy based on import substitution has lost its appeal everywhere. The view that integration into the emerging global economy is the best available road to prosperity had, and still has, substantial support among policy-makers in most developing countries. Implementation of trade liberalization policies, moreover, often brought other

[1] For review and analysis of these developments, see Campa and Goldberg (1997); Feenstra (1998); Yeats (2001); and Hummels, Ishii and Yi (2001).

[2] It should be noted that TNCs are not new; they started emerging in the eighteenth century and have since been engaged in production and exports of primary commodities in many parts of the developing world. But they now have a new role: the development of global production systems, primarily in manufacturing. See, for example, Wilkins (1998) and Oxfam (2002).

[3] See UNCTAD (2000), p. 4, table 1.1.

[4] See World Bank (2001), p. 55, figure 2.1; Oxfam (2002), p. 124, figure 5.1; and Bourguignon et al. (2002), Ch. 2.

changes in its wake. Most countries, for example, adopted policies designed to attract foreign direct investment (FDI).[5] Many also sought to increase the role of the market (and to reduce correspondingly the role of the state) in the economy through privatization programmes.

Together, these changes not only stimulated flows of trade and capital across countries but also altered the character of trade between North and South. A key proposition presented and developed in this book is that growth of North–South trade in competing products is the genuinely new feature that distinguishes the current process of globalization from the earlier episodes.

Before elaborating on the proposition, however, we would like to emphasize three points. First, all the changes notwithstanding, we are far from being in an era of free flows of trade and capital.[6] Trade liberalization had quite different points of departure in different countries and the pace of liberalization also varied across countries. Tariff rates still remain high in large parts of the world. Moreover, low average tariff rates often conceal high tariff rates on particular items of import. Though the average tariff rates in industrialized countries are very low, for example, the tariff rates on imports of agricultural products and labour-intensive manufactures are actually quite high. Besides, new types of non-tariff barriers to trade, such as anti-dumping measures, have been on the rise.[7] Thus the only assertion that can be made at this stage is that flows of trade and capital are significantly freer today than they were two decades ago. And the trend towards freer trade looks likely to continue; at the time of writing a new round of trade negotiations under the auspices of the World Trade Organization (WTO) is in progress.

Second, there has been no liberalization of cross-border labour flow; international labour mobility remains low and there are no signs of South–North migration growing. This stands in sharp contrast to what happened during the earlier globalization period (1870–1913) when around 60 million Europeans migrated to the New World (Argentina, Australia, Brazil, Canada, New Zealand and the United States). However, as we shall see later (in Chapter 5), it is not that there has been no change in this area. The industrialized countries have in fact taken steps to encourage immigration of high-skilled labour from developing countries. Independently of policies, moreover, freer flows of trade and capital have generated incentives for South–North migration

[5] See UNCTAD (2000), p. 6, table 1.3.

[6] This needs to be emphasized because the debate on globalization is turning into a debate on free trade. Two recent books, for example, are devoted to presenting the case for free trade: Bhagwati (2002) and Irwin (2002). There is no need to think, however, that globalization confronts us with a stark choice between free trade and autarky.

[7] See World Bank (2001), Ch. 2; World Bank (2002), Ch. 2; UNCTAD (2002), Ch. 4; Oxfam (2002), Ch. 4; and Tharakan (2000).

of high-skilled labour and disincentives for South–North migration of low-skilled labour. International mobility of high-skilled labour is on the rise and concerns about "brain drain" are resurfacing.

Finally, the fact that national policies have played an important role in promoting globalization means that, contrary to widely held belief, the process is neither inevitable nor irreversible. Globalization has been reversed before and can be reversed again. Whether the current process of globalization continues to progress or comes to a halt depends ultimately on the political acceptability of its consequences by populations in nation states. And this acceptability in turn depends on how the international community manages the process of globalization as much as on how national policies are adapted to it. The impression that the "uncontrollable" force of globalization has robbed nation states of policy-making authority is widespread but incorrect. It owes its existence to the fact that national governments, while introducing unpopular policies, have often found it convenient to plead helplessness in the face of globalization. The impression distracts attention from questions that ought to be seriously addressed and debated. Is a retreat into protectionism desirable? If not, how should globalization proceed and how should national policies be adapted?

Globalization: An empirical sketch

Throughout history, trade has been a far more consistent mechanism of international economic interaction than cross-border movement of capital or labour. It comes as no surprise, therefore, that the process of global integration of product markets is much more advanced than that of capital or labour markets, a fact that is brought out by figures 2.1 and 2.2 together with table 2.1. Towards the end of the 1990s, world trade in goods and services constituted 47 per cent of world GDP, while the flow of FDI constituted just over 2 per cent of world GDP. Even the total stock of FDI constituted only 14 per cent of world GDP in 1998. And the stock of migrant population, not surprisingly, constituted just 2.4 per cent of the world population in 1998. This broad picture tells us why, in the literature, growth of trade has been regarded as the driving force for globalization. There are other reasons too. On the whole, trade is significantly freer than capital flow (which in turn is much freer than cross-border labour flow). Moreover, as we shall see below, trade and FDI flow are not unrelated; FDI flow promotes trade. It is also important to recognize that integration of product markets implies a certain degree of integration of factor markets (even when the factors are immobile across national frontiers), but the latter does not imply the former.

Table 2.1 Capital and labour mobility, 1980 and 1998

	1980	1998
Stock of FDI as % of GDP, world	5.0	14.0
Stock of migrant population as % of total population, world	2.2	2.4

Source: UNCTAD (2000), p. 319, Annex table B6, and Ghose (2002).

When we look at the trends, it is immediately clear that there was a definite break in the time-path of the FDI–GDP ratio in the mid-1980s; the importance of FDI flow in the world economy grew much more rapidly after the mid-1980s than before. This is reflected in the fact that FDI stock as a percentage of GDP increased quite dramatically, from 5 in 1980 to 14 in 1998. But a similar pattern is not observed in the case of the trade–GDP ratio; this first declined, then rose to reach the 1980 level in 1992, and grew rapidly only thereafter. This appears a little puzzling at first. But the puzzle is not difficult to resolve. For figure 2.1 also shows a break in the ratio of manufactured trade to GDP in the mid-1980s, though not perhaps as dramatic as in the case of FDI flow shown in figure 2.2. It can be said, then, that there has been an accelerated growth of both manufactured trade and FDI flow since the mid-1980s. Given that widespread trade liberalization also occurred in the period since the mid-1980s, it is reasonable to suppose that trade liberalization triggered this accelerated growth. This is why the mid-1980s are widely regarded as the beginning of the current process of globalization. The missing element in this process, of course, is cross-border flow of labour. The world's migrant population as a percentage of the total population barely increased; it was 2.2 in 1980 and 2.4 in 1998.

It is already clear that globalization is not only about growth of world trade but also about important changes in its structure, and this can usefully be made more explicit. As table 2.2 shows, only the first half of the 1980s saw rapid growth of trade in services. From the mid-1980s onwards, the share of services trade in total trade (in goods and services) showed a mildly declining trend. The most significant change after the mid-1980s was in the structure of merchandise (goods) trade: trade in manufactures increased sharply, while that in primary commodities (including petroleum products) basically stagnated. By the end of the 1990s, trade in manufactures accounted for nearly two-thirds of total trade in goods and services and close to 80 per cent of total merchandise trade.

Rapid expansion of trade in manufactures has thus been a central feature of globalization and certain implications of this fact are worth noting. First, it seems to provide empirical support for what, in economic literature, is known as the Prebisch–Singer hypothesis.[8] As global income has grown, the global demand for primary commodities has grown at a decelerating rate while that for manufactures has grown at an accelerating rate. A stage seems to have been reached now where global income growth generates increased demand principally for manufactures. It is true, of course, that trade in non-petroleum primary commodities is much less liberalized than trade in manufactures and this

Figure 2.1 World trade as a percentage of world GDP, 1980–98

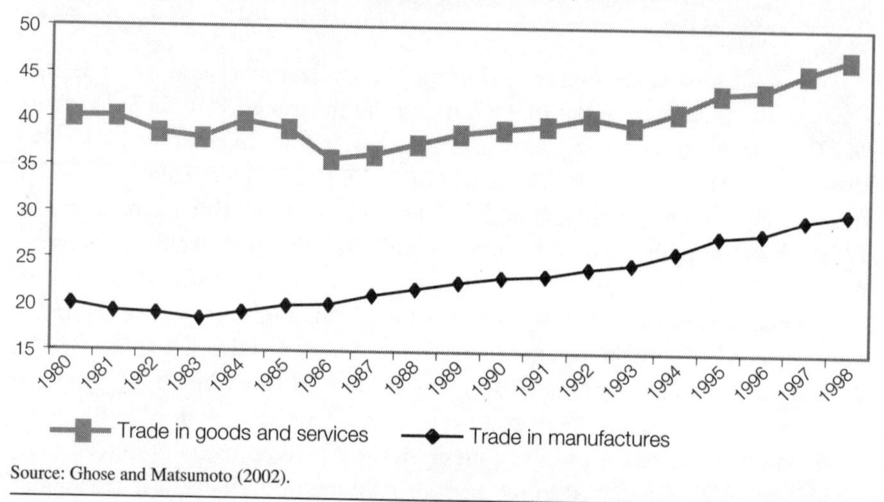

Source: Ghose and Matsumoto (2002).

Figure 2.2 Foreign direct investment flow as a percentage of world GDP, 1980–98

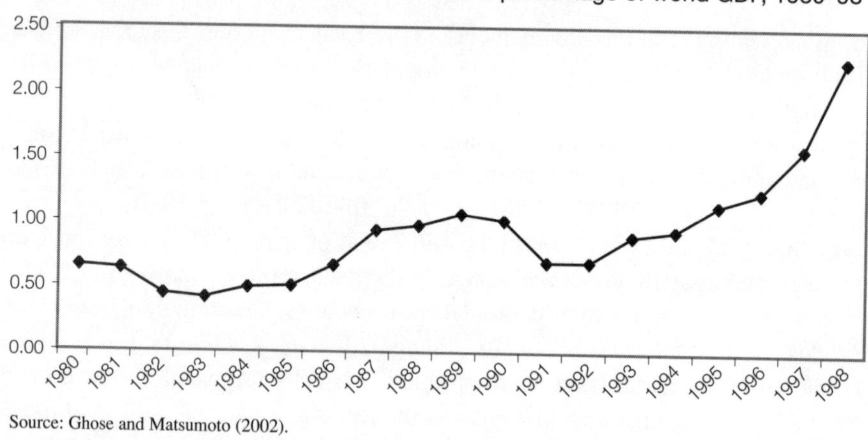

Source: Ghose and Matsumoto (2002).

[8] This was formulated, independently, by Prebisch (1959) and Singer (1950), and provided a strong argument for import-substitution industrialization in developing countries. Prebisch's ideas were originally put forward in ECLA (1950).

Table 2.2 Structure of world trade (% share)

	Services	Merchandise	Manufactures	Non-petroleum primary commodities	Petroleum products
1980	11.0	89.0	49.7	23.8	15.5
1985	21.8	78.2	50.8	15.7	11.7
1991	21.4	78.6	58.7	12.9	7.0
1998	19.9	80.1	64.2	11.5	4.4

Source: Ghose and Matsumoto (2002).

must have had something to do with the stagnation of the former. But it would be surprising if this were the only reason for the change in the structure of merchandise trade. Second, the most direct and significant labour market effects of globalization are expected to be those of trade on manufacturing employment and wages. This has special significance for developing countries, where improvement of employment conditions requires transfer of labour from agriculture to manufacturing. In industrialized countries, on the other hand, a process of labour transfer from manufacturing into services (a process known as deindustrialization) has been under way since the early 1970s; as such, labour market effects of globalization should in principle be much less significant than in developing countries.

A closer examination shows that the rapid expansion of world trade in manufactures created real opportunities for developing countries to transform themselves into significant exporters of manufactures. Traditionally, trade between industrialized and developing countries has been, for the main, in non-competing products, with industrialized countries exporting manufactures and developing countries exporting primary commodities. Globalization is in the process of altering this pattern, as table 2.3 shows. Between the early 1980s and the late 1990s, the share of industrialized countries in world manufactured exports declined from 83 per cent to 71 per cent, while the share of developing countries grew from 12 per cent to 26 per cent (the share of transition countries (TC) fell from 5 per cent to 3 per cent). The share of manufactured exports in total merchandise exports increased for all countries, reflecting the general rise in the importance of manufactures in world trade; but the increase was dramatic only in the case of developing countries.

In contrast to the past, therefore, trade between industrialized and developing countries is now increasingly in competing products; this is the most significant development since the early 1980s and constitutes the distinguishing

Table 2.3 Manufactured exports, 1980–82 and 1996–98

	% share in world manufactured exports		Manufactured exports as % of merchandise exports	
	1980–82	1996–98	1980–82	1996–98
Industrialized countries	83.3	71.2	71.6	79.9
Developing countries	12.0	25.9	22.4	65.8
European transition countries	4.7	2.9	45.9	53.2

Note: The total number of countries, territories, areas and regions considered is 162, of which 23 are industrialized, 131 developing and 8 in transition. For full lists, see Appendix 2.1.

Source: Ghose and Matsumoto (2002).

feature of the current process of globalization. The story does not end here, however. For manufacturing capability was (and still is) unevenly distributed across developing countries. Globalization, consequently, set in motion a process of polarization of developing countries into two categories – exporters of manufactures and exporters of primary commodities. An inspection of the data shows that only certain developing countries succeeded in shifting their export base from primary commodities to manufactures; for the rest, the old pattern of trade with industrialized countries remained basically unaltered.

In table 2.4, the developing countries are classified into three categories, on the basis of export structure. Manufactures-exporting developing countries (ME) are those for which manufactured exports constituted, by 1998, at least 50 per cent of merchandise exports.[9] The rest of the developing countries are then classified into those that are major petroleum exporters (PE) and those that are not (DC). The growing polarization of developing countries is evident from table 2.4. It shows that what appears to be a change in the pattern of North–South trade is in essence a change in the pattern of trade between industrialized countries and a group of 24 developing countries. This group achieved a dramatic increase in its share of world exports of manufactures, from about 11 per cent in the early 1980s to about 25 per cent in the late 1990s. By the late 1990s, the group accounted for more than 95 per cent of manufactured exports from the developing world and the structure of its merchandise exports was very similar to that of industrialized countries. The rest of the developing world (PE and DC), in contrast, remained overwhelmingly dependent on exports of primary commodities.

[9] Three countries – Argentina, Egypt and Indonesia – have been included in the group even though the share of manufactured exports in total merchandise exports had not quite reached 50 per cent by 1998 in their case. Throughout this book, manufactures are so defined as to exclude non-ferrous metals.

Table 2.4 Trade in manufactures, developing countries, 1980–82 and 1996–98

	% share in world manufactured exports		Manufactured exports as % of merchandise exports	
	1980–82	1996–98	1980–82	1996–98
ME	10.8	24.8	44.6	79.6
PE	0.5	0.4	1.9	7.8
DC	0.7	0.7	12.3	26.2
All developing countries	12.0	25.9	22.4	65.8

Note: ME – manufactures-exporting developing countries (24); PE – petroleum-exporting developing countries (17); DC – other developing countries (90). For full lists, see Appendix 2.1.

Source: Ghose and Matsumoto (2002).

Moreover, as table 2.5 shows, the ME countries have been expanding their share of export markets in manufactures everywhere. In other words, manufactures from ME countries are increasingly in competition with manufactures from industrialized (ID) countries in all parts of the world. Of particular interest is the fact that, in relative terms, the importance of ME countries as exporters of manufactures to ID countries is on the rise and the importance of ID countries as exporters of manufactures to ME countries is on the decline. A real change in the international division of labour is evidently under way.

As suggested above, in a world where trade expansion has been occurring mainly in manufactures, the effect of trade liberalization on trade performance of developing countries is most likely to have been dependent on their capacity

Table 2.5 Percentage distribution of manufactured imports by source region, 1980–82 and 1996–98

Source region	Importing region							
	ID		ME		PE		DC	
	1980–82	1996–98	1980–82	1996–98	1980–82	1996–98	1980–82	1996–98
ID	87.0	74.8	82.3	62.2	85.2	74.3	79.6	62.7
ME	10.3	21.4	15.8	36.5	9.2	22.0	13.0	29.8
PE	0.4	0.7	0.6	0.5	1.8	1.8	1.1	1.5
DC	0.1	0.3	0.4	0.5	0.9	1.8	3.7	1.5
TC	2.2	2.8	0.9	0.3	2.9	0.1	2.6	4.5

Source: Ghose and Matsumoto (2002).

Table 2.6 Trade performance, 1980 and 1998

	Manufactured exports as % of merchandise exports		Merchandise trade as % of GDP		% share in world merchandise trade	
	1980	1998	1980	1998	1980	1998
ID	71.6	79.9	31.0	32.6	66.5	66.9
ME	44.6	79.6	32.1	50.9	13.7	23.3
PE	1.9	7.8	74.0	67.5	10.6	3.0
DC	12.3	26.2	40.9	46.8	4.6	2.6
TC	45.9	53.2	48.7	59.8	5.2	4.2

Source: Ghose and Matsumoto (2002).

to produce and export manufactures. This is confirmed by table 2.6, which also highlights the phenomenon of global exclusion (or "marginalization", to use a more familiar term). The table shows that those developing countries that were able to expand manufactured exports were also able to increase their participation in global trade much more substantially than others. Those developing countries that remained dependent on exports of primary commodities faced global exclusion in the sense that they became increasingly insignificant players in the global market place. By the late 1990s, 23 industrialized countries and 24 developing countries together accounted for more than 90 per cent of world merchandise trade. The other 107 developing countries (including the petroleum exporters), which accounted for less than 6 per cent of world merchandise trade, had clearly become marginal to the global economy.

Global exclusion is one of the most undesirable features of the current process of globalization, and we shall have many occasions to touch upon the problem throughout the book. But there are two particular points that we should note here. First, exclusion has been a characteristic feature of all episodes of globalization. The globalization of 1870–1913 included only the countries of Western Europe and of the New World (Argentina, Australia, Canada, New Zealand and the United States). The post-war integration included, additionally, Japan and the countries of Southern Europe. Clearly, global exclusion is not a particular feature of the current process of globalization; what is particular is the widespread concern about the problem. Second, though global exclusion resulted partly from non-liberalization of trade in many primary commodities, its root cause lay in the lack of preparedness of many developing countries for participation in manufactured trade. The globally excluded developing countries had not pursued coherent industrialization strategies in periods prior

Table 2.7 Trade and FDI flow, 1980 and 1998

	% share in global FDI inflow		% share in world merchandise trade	
	1980	1998	1980	1998
ID	68.0	62.2	66.5	66.9
ME	19.5	25.8	13.7	23.3
PE	7.9	2.0	10.6	3.0
DC	4.6	5.8	4.0	2.8
TC	0.0	4.2	5.2	4.2

Source: Ghose and Matsumoto (2002).

to the opening up of their economies. Many of them also lacked the minimum infrastructure – physical (for example, transport and communication facilities, electricity) and social (for example, education, health, legal framework, institutions of financial and labour market institutions) – required for manufacturing production in competitive conditions. These deficiencies made it difficult for them to shift their export base away from primary commodities even in the face of stagnation in world demand for these commodities. The point is important, for we need to recognize that liberalization of trade in primary commodities, desirable though it is, cannot be the miracle cure for the problem of global exclusion. Overcoming the problem will require reducing the dependence of the excluded countries on exports of primary commodities.

Before concluding this sketch, it is useful to look at some evidence in support of the proposition that trade and FDI go together and reinforce each other. The data presented in table 2.7 show a remarkable correspondence between a country group's share in world merchandise trade and its share in global FDI flow. The industrialized countries account for a very large part of global FDI flow just as they account for a very large part of world merchandise trade. Though the total share of the developing countries in global FDI flow rose between the early 1980s and the late 1990s, this can be explained by the sharp increase in FDI flow to manufactures-exporting developing countries. In the late 1990s, 23 industrialized countries and 24 developing countries (ME countries) together received 88 per cent of global FDI flow, while the rest of the developing world received just about 8 per cent. Global exclusion is as visible in the context of FDI as it is in the context of trade.[10]

[10] It will be recalled that the European transition countries (TC), which have also become rather marginal to the world economy and are also affected by globalization, are excluded from of our discussions because of the systemic transformation under way in these economies.

Globalization: Then and now

The current process of globalization is often compared to an earlier episode that is known to have occurred during 1870–1913. Such comparisons are helpful principally in identifying the distinctive characteristics of the current process. A good deal of research has by now been carried out and it is fairly clear that, despite some superficial similarities, there are quite fundamental differences between the two episodes of globalization.[11] Here we note some of the main results of this research, results that highlight the particularities of the current process and facilitate the analysis that follows.

Like the current process, the earlier process of globalization was characterized by rapid growth of trade and capital flow. For most of today's industrialized countries, the ratio of merchandise trade to GDP increased rapidly and, by 1913, reached levels that were surpassed only in the 1990s for some and are yet to be overtaken for others.[12] The stock of FDI worldwide is estimated to have reached over 9 per cent of world GDP by 1913, a figure that was surpassed only in the second half of the 1990s.[13] There is also evidence to show that, as in the current process of globalization, FDI played a major role in stimulating trade. But similarities between the two episodes of globalization end here. Differences, on the other hand, are many. Here we choose to highlight the following.

First, unlike in the current phase, trade liberalization did not play a major role in promoting globalization in the earlier period. In fact, among the European and New World countries (which were the chief players in the globalization process), free trade was a preoccupation of the United Kingdom alone. Tariff rates were reduced in some countries (mainly in Europe) during 1860–80 but remained high in others, particularly in the United States. After 1880, tariff rates were growing in virtually all the countries concerned.[14] Particularly during 1880–1913, trade and FDI flow grew despite declining openness, not because of increasing openness. The 1870–1913 globalization was effectively triggered by the dramatically declining cost and growing ease of transport.

Second, the bulk of the trade was in primary products; indeed, growth of trade in primary products could be said to have been the driving force for globalization during the period. By 1913, trade in primary products accounted for 64 per cent of merchandise trade. The bulk of the FDI also went into the

[11] See Bairoch and Kozul-Wright (1998); Crafts (2000); and Sachs and Warner (1995).

[12] See Crafts (2000), p. 26, table 2.1; and Bairoch and Kozul-Wright (1998), p. 42, table 1.1.

[13] See Bairoch and Kozul-Wright (1998), p. 46.

[14] On the other hand, several Asian countries – China, Japan, India, Indonesia, Korea and Thailand – were forced to moved to free trade through either colonial domination or "gunboat diplomacy". See Bourguignon et al. (2002), p. 19, and Milanovic (2002).

production of primary commodities and into infrastructure needed for transport of primary commodities. All this was linked to the establishment of an international division of labour whereby the major European nations exported manufactures to and imported primary commodities from the rest of the world. Nations were trading in non-competing products and it was this kind of trade that was growing. It is an important fact that this was actually a period of deindustrialization for most of today's developing countries, which then were colonies of the dominant European powers. The globalization of 1870–1913 was in fact far less inclusive than the current process.

Finally, international migration was a prominent feature of the earlier episode of globalization (see Chapter 5 below). As already noted, around 60 million Europeans migrated to the New World during the period. For several European countries, emigration was large and sustained enough to make growth rates of population and labour force insignificant or negative for years. The immigration rate into the United States, the principal destination for European migrants, rose from 6.4 per thousand of native population in 1870 to 10.4 per thousand in 1910. The corresponding figure for 1990 was just 2.6, and this is illustrative of the contrast between then and now.

Globalization: Issues and concerns

As demonstrated above, the key characteristic of the current process of globalization is the growth of trade in competing products (i.e., manufactures) between industrialized and a group of developing countries. For the first time in history, there is North–South competition in the global product market (traditionally, the competition has been North–North and South–South). The key effect of this competition is a redistribution of manufacturing production and hence of manufacturing employment between North and South. This is not a zero-sum game, for global manufacturing output and employment are not fixed but growing. But redistribution is significant nevertheless, as can be seen from table 2.8. These data on manufacturing employment, derived from ILO and United Nations Industrial Development Organization (UNIDO) sources, suffer from a number of important limitations. They leave out, in all cases, the employment in household and micro enterprises. Besides, the coverage is not uniform across countries: in a few cases, important segments of the manufacturing sector were left out of account, and for quite a number of countries no data are available. Despite these limitations, however, the broad patterns of redistribution suggested by the data are, in our judgement, fairly accurate.

Two observations can be made on the basis of these data. First, global manufacturing employment is being redistributed away from both the

Table 2.8 Global redistribution of manufacturing employment, 1980 and 1997

	In millions		As % of total	
	1980	1997	1980	1997
ID (21 countries)	66.6	54.6	37.0	30.9
ME (22 countries and regions)	64.4	93.4	35.8	53.0
ID + ME	**131.0**	**148.0**	**72.8**	**83.9**
PE (6 countries)	1.0	1.0	0.6	0.6
DC (28 countries and regions)	2.3	2.8	1.3	1.6
TC (7 countries and regions)	45.5	24.5	25.3	13.9
All (84 countries and regions)	**179.8**	**176.3**	**100.0**	**100.0**

Note: For lists of countries, see Appendix 2.1.

Source: Ghose and Matsumoto (2002).

industrialized countries and the European transition countries towards the manufactures-exporting developing countries. Second, global manufacturing employment actually declined (for the whole group of 84 countries, the aggregate employment declined at an annual rate of 0.1 per cent).

It is arguable, however, that a more accurate view of the effect of globalization emerges if we confine attention to just the industrialized and the manufactures-exporting developing countries. The sharp decline of manufacturing employment in the European transition countries probably has much more to do with the systemic transformation that is under way in those countries than with globalization. And developing countries other than the manufactures-exporters are of marginal significance anyway. If we take these considerations into account, we can say that the employment redistribution has been occurring mainly between the industrialized countries and the manufactures-exporting developing countries. We can also say that the gain in the latter is much larger than the loss in the former. It needs to be said, however, that the figures in table 2.8 overstate the redistribution that is attributable to globalization. For even without globalization, manufacturing employment would have declined in the industrialized countries (where a process of deindustrialization had been under way since the early 1970s) and would have increased in the manufactures-exporting developing countries (which had been pursuing industrialization for a fairly long period prior to globalization). Nevertheless, there is no doubt that redistribution of global manufacturing employment between the industrialized countries and a group of developing countries has been a key effect of globalization.

The issues and concerns about globalization are, in essence, about the economic and social consequences of this process of global redistribution of manufacturing employment and of the changing pattern of trade that has induced the redistribution. For the purposes of analysis in this book, we focus on the following four major areas of concern.[15]

First, at a global level, the changing pattern of trade has clearly had differential impact on the trade performance of countries. There are gainers and losers; the already noted problem of global exclusion is one relevant indicator. Since trade performance influences economic growth, globalization has altered the growth trajectories of countries. This means that globalization has had an impact on global income inequality. The question is whether this impact is positive or negative. There is widespread concern today that the poorer countries are systematically the losers and the richer countries are systematically the gainers. If this is the case, it would follow that globalization has had the effect of exacerbating the already huge inequality among nations.

Second, the redistribution of manufacturing employment, induced by globalization, means (as we have seen) that manufacturing employment and wages have been affected in both industrialized and developing countries. There are concerns that these effects may have been adverse in both types of countries. In industrialized countries, the employment of low-skilled labour has declined and the wage differential between high-skilled and low-skilled labour has increased; growing trade with low-income countries is often blamed for these labour market developments. In the case of manufactures-exporting developing countries, the key concern is about quality of jobs. Growing openness and trade simultaneously destroy (in import-competing industries) and create (in export-oriented industries) jobs. Even when more jobs are created than destroyed, as appears to be the case, it is possible that the jobs destroyed are of a higher quality than the jobs created. In this case, there is a worsening of job quality and this is what, many suspect, has been happening. Moreover, contrary to expectation, the skill premium has shown a rising trend in some of these countries and this too is a source of concern.

Third, that there has been no liberalization of international migration is itself a matter of some concern since it thwarts the development of an international labour market. Even in the absence of such liberalization, moreover, it seems unlikely that a process of global redistribution of output and employment will leave cross-border labour mobility unaffected. As we shall see, globalization has in fact increased the mobility of skilled workers and reduced the

[15] This, to be sure, is not an exhaustive list of the concerns. We have chosen simply to focus on those concerns that relate to employment, wages and incomes.

mobility of unskilled workers. In other words, globalization may not have increased the magnitude of international migration but it has changed its character. The primary concern here is that "brain drain" may have been increasing and that this could have harmful consequences for long-term growth of developing countries.

Finally, there is widespread apprehension that competition in trade and for attracting FDI may be leading to a lowering of labour standards worldwide. In other words, globalization may have set in motion a "race to the bottom". It is this fear that has prompted the demand for incorporation of labour standards into trade agreements (the so-called "social clause"). There are ambiguities about the nature of the problem, however, and the basis for the fear remains to be properly defined.

The chapters that follow examine whether and to what extent there are valid theoretical and empirical grounds for the concerns.

Appendix 2.1

List of countries[16]

The full list of countries and regions used for the empirical analysis is as follows.

Industrialized countries (ID): Australia, Austria, Belgium, Canada, Denmark, Finland, France, Germany, Greece, Iceland, Ireland, Italy, Japan, Luxembourg, Netherlands, New Zealand, Norway, Portugal, Spain, Sweden, Switzerland, United Kingdom, United States (23)

Manufactures-exporting developing countries (ME): Argentina, Bangladesh, Brazil, China, Egypt, Hong Kong (China), India, Indonesia, Israel, Korea (Republic), Malaysia, Malta, Mauritius, Mexico, Morocco, Pakistan, Philippines, Singapore, South Africa, Sri Lanka, Taiwan (China), Thailand, Tunisia, Turkey (24)

Petroleum-exporting developing countries (PE): Algeria, Angola, Bahrain, Brunei, Cameroon, Ecuador, Gabon, Iran (Islamic Republic), Iraq, Kuwait, Libyan Arab Jamahiriya, Nigeria, Oman, Qatar, Saudi Arabia, United Arab Emirates, Venezuela (17)

Other developing countries (DC): Afghanistan, Bahamas, Barbados, Belize, Benin, Bermuda, Bhutan, Bolivia, British Indian Ocean Territory, Burkina Faso, Burundi, Cambodia, Cayman Islands, Central African Republic, Chad, Chile, Colombia, Comoros, Congo (Republic), Congo (Democratic Republic), Costa Rica, Côte d'Ivoire, Cuba, Djibouti, Dominican Republic, El Salvador, Equatorial Guinea, Ethiopia, Falkland Islands, Fiji, French Guiana, Gambia, Ghana, Greenland, Guadeloupe, Guatemala, Guinea, Guinea-Bissau, Guyana, Haiti, Honduras, Jamaica, Jordan, Kenya, Kiribati, Korea (Democratic People's Republic), Lao People's Democratic Republic, Lebanon, Liberia, Madagascar, Malawi, Maldives, Mali, Mauritania, Mongolia, Mozambique, Myanmar, Nepal, Netherlands Antilles, New Caledonia, Nicaragua, Niger, Panama, Papua New Guinea, Paraguay, Peru, Réunion, Rwanda, Senegal, Seychelles, Sierra Leone, Solomon Islands, Somalia, Saint Helena, Saint Kitts and Nevis, Saint Pierre and Miquelon, Sudan, Suriname, Syrian Arab Republic, Tanzania (United Republic), Togo, Trinidad and Tobago, Turks and Caicos Islands, Uganda, Uruguay, Viet Nam, Western Sahara, Yemen, Zambia, Zimbabwe (90)

[16] This list includes territories, areas and regions.

Transition countries (TC): Albania, Bulgaria, Former Czechoslovakia, Hungary, Poland, Romania, Former Yugoslavia, Former USSR (8)

Trade statistics are available for all these 162 countries and regions. But data on many other variables are not available for all of them. For analysis of specific issues in different parts of the book, specific subsamples (of this universe of 162) are used, although there is a core set of countries (accounting for a large majority of the world population) that is common to all the subsamples.

Statistics on manufacturing employment, as mentioned in the text, are available for only 84 countries and regions. The countries that *are not included* are as follows.

ID: Belgium, Switzerland (2)

ME: Bangladesh, Tunisia (2)

PE: Angola, Brunei, Gabon, Iran (Islamic Republic), Iraq, Libyan Arab Jamahiriya, Nigeria, Oman, Qatar, Saudi Arabia, United Arab Emirates (11)

DC: Afghanistan, Belize, Benin, Bermuda, Bhutan, British Indian Ocean Territory, Burkina Faso, Burundi, Cambodia, Cayman Islands, Chad, Comoros, Congo (Republic), Congo (Democratic Republic), Côte d'Ivoire, Cuba, Djibouti, Dominican Republic, Equatorial Guinea, Ethiopia, Falkland Islands, French Guiana, Gambia, Ghana, Greenland, Guadeloupe, Guinea, Guinea-Bissau, Guyana, Haiti, Kiribati, Korea (Democratic People's Republic), Lao People's Democratic Republic, Lebanon, Liberia, Maldives, Mali, Mauritania, Mongolia, Mozambique, Myanmar, Nepal, New Caledonia, Niger, Papua New Guinea, Paraguay, Réunion, Rwanda, Seychelles, Sierra Leone, Somalia, Saint Helena, Saint Kitts and Nevis, Saint Pierre and Miquelon, Sudan, Tanzania, Turks and Caicos Islands, Uganda, Viet Nam, Western Sahara, Yemen, Zambia (62)

TC: Albania (1)

3 TRADE AND GLOBAL INCOME INEQUALITY

Introduction

The gap in per capita income between the richest and the poorest countries of the world has been steadily growing for a long time, at least since the last quarter of the eighteenth century. We know that the process was triggered by the industrial revolution and sharpened by the globalization of 1870–1913.[1] But the process continued through the years between the First and the Second World Wars, a period that saw a progressive reversal of globalization. And it seems to have continued through the second half of the twentieth century.[2]

While economists have long been aware of this unwelcome trend, popular concern about global inequality is of recent origin and it is legitimate to wonder why. One reason is the sharp growth of travel and information flow brought about by the fairly recent advances in transport and communication technologies; this has increased popular awareness of the huge differences in living conditions between rich and poor countries of the world. Another reason is widespread exposure to the disparity in working conditions and purchasing power of workers and consumers in different countries through the growing North–South trade in competing commodities. In addition there is unease about the expansion of transnational conglomerates, which are popularly viewed in industrialized countries as both the cause and the evidence of the enormous divide between the "haves" and "have-nots". The combination of these factors heightens awareness of the income gap and focuses attention on globalization as a common threat. In popular perception, therefore, the widening gap in per capita income between the richest and the poorest countries appears to be a relatively recent phenomenon linked to the current process of globalization, and one that is the concern of all.

[1] See, for example, Crafts (2000), and Bourguignon and Morrisson (2002).

[2] "The income gap between the fifth of the world's people living in the richest countries and the fifth in the poorest was 74 to 1 in 1997, up from 60 to 1 in 1990 and 30 to 1 in 1960." UNDP (1999), p. 3.

The popular concern is a welcome development, but the underlying perception is based on a rather incomplete understanding of the issues involved. The notion of global income inequality is in fact more complex than appears at first sight, and the gap in per capita income between the richest and the poorest countries is neither the only nor the best indicator of this inequality. In other words, a widening gap in per capita income between the richest and the poorest countries does not necessarily indicate growth of global income inequality. And the fact that such a widening has been a long-term trend rather than a recent development should warn us against any quick judgement that the widening has been caused by globalization.

In this chapter, we seek to answer empirically two questions.[3] First, has global income inequality been growing since the onset of the current period of globalization? To answer this question, we need to examine closely the notion of global income inequality and to consider methods of measurement. Second, how has trade liberalization – the *primum mobile* of globalization – affected global income inequality? To answer this question, we shall need to consider the effects of trade liberalization on the trade performance of countries, as well as the linkage between trade performance and economic growth.

Global income inequality, 1981–97

The preliminaries

Global income inequality can be conceptualized in three possible ways. The first way is to consider the distribution of countries by per capita GDP and the inequality revealed by this distribution. We shall call this *inter-country* inequality. It is this notion that is implicitly adopted when the gap in per capita income between the richest and the poorest countries is taken as an indicator of global income inequality. The weakness of this approach lies in the fact that the per capita GDP of China is accorded no more importance than that of the Gambia even though the former clearly affects a vastly larger segment of the world population. If the gap in per capita GDP between the United States and China narrows while that between the United States and the Gambia widens, we would still conclude that global income inequality has risen, and this does not seem right.

Recognition of this problem leads us to consider a second way of defining global income inequality. Here we focus on the distribution of the world population by per capita GDP and the inequality revealed by this distribution. We shall call

[3] The analysis presented in the rest of the chapter is based on a recent ILO study, Ghose (2001). See also Ghose (forthcoming).

this *international* inequality. If the gap in per capita GDP between the United States and China narrows while that between the United States and the Gambia widens, we shall now conclude that global income inequality has declined, and this seems right. This also tells us that there are good reasons for preferring the notion of *international* inequality to that of *inter-country* inequality.

However, per capita GDP of a country is not the income of each of the inhabitants of that country. Income distribution is unequal in each country, and the notion of *international* inequality leaves this fact out of account. The third – and most satisfactory – notion of global income inequality is one that reflects the distribution of persons, irrespective of their country of residence, by "income received". We shall call this *world income distribution.*

Though inequality of *world income distribution* is the most satisfactory notion of global income inequality, we shall not attempt any analysis of the trend in this inequality in this chapter for two important reasons. The first reason is the non-availability of adequate statistical information. Data on within-country income distribution are simply not available for many countries. Even the data that are available suffer from serious limitations. In particular, because of differences in definition, sampling method and coverage of population, the data are often not comparable either across countries or over time.[4] All this means that it is extremely difficult to establish any robust conclusion about the trend in the inequality of *world income distribution.* Recent research has made good progress in overcoming many of the difficulties,[5] but much more research is clearly required.

The second reason is analytical. The mechanisms through which trade might affect *world income distribution* are not particularly well understood. Thus even if it were possible to establish the trend, it would still be very difficult to determine if trade liberalization had anything to do with it.[6]

Our analysis in this chapter, therefore, focuses on the first two notions of global income inequality, namely, *inter-country* inequality and *international* inequality.[7] The period covered is 1981–97. The data are derived from United Nations and World Bank sources. The choice of the period is dictated by two

---

[4] See Deininger and Squire (1996) and Li, Squire and Zou (1998) for discussions of the limitations of the data.

[5] See, in particular, Milanovic (2000); Bourguignon and Morrisson (2002); and Sala-i-Martin (2002).

[6] It should be said, however, that changes in *international* inequality are the most important determinants of changes in inequality of *world income distribution.* Except over a very long period, changes in country-level inequalities are usually small and have only a minor effect on changes in *world income distribution.* In general, the trend in *international* inequality is a good indicator of the trend in *world income distribution.*

[7] It is worth noting that, if we place our faith in the available data on country-level income distribution, we have to conclude that income inequality has been rising in most countries of the world over the last two decades (see Appendix 3.2). However, it cannot be deduced from this that global income inequality has also been rising. We should also note that Li, Squire and Zou (1998), who have painstakingly checked the data for reliability and comparability, find that there are as many cases of rising inequality as there are of declining inequality.

considerations. First, since we wish to study the linkage between globalization and global income inequality, we need to choose a period that is widely regarded as the period of globalization. Second, since all the required data are not available for all the countries of the world, we are constrained to choosing a sample. But in order to produce credible results, we need to include as many countries as possible in our sample. We are in a position to assemble together the required data for 96 countries (which accounted for 84 per cent of the world population in 1997) for the period 1981–97. Attempts to extend the period beyond 1997 would have significantly reduced the number of countries covered, as up-to-date data on several variables are not available for quite a few of the countries. Our sample excludes, by choice, the transition countries of Eastern Europe and Central Asia and the very small countries (those with a population of less than 0.5 million in 1981). It also excludes Taiwan (China) and Germany, as adequate data were not available to us.[8]

Inter-country inequality, 1981–97

It is useful to start by noting that standard economic theory actually predicts a steady decline in *inter-country* inequality over time. An enduring idea in growth theory has been the so-called "catching-up" or "convergence" hypothesis. This says that less developed countries should grow faster than more developed countries so that per capita incomes across countries should show a tendency to converge. The hypothesis is based on three theoretical arguments. First, less developed countries enjoy an advantage in that they can simply adopt and exploit technologies that more developed countries had to develop through their own efforts. Second, a standard assumption in growth theory is that of diminishing returns to factor inputs. This says that, *ceteris paribus*, the productivity of a factor declines as more of it is used. To the extent that the assumption is valid, the productivity of capital should be higher in less developed economies, which are capital-scarce. For equivalent rates of investment, therefore, less developed economies should grow faster than more developed economies. Third, the process of economic growth involves transfer of labour from less productive to more productive activities and such transfers by themselves increase the average labour productivity in the economy. Since less developed economies have a higher proportion of the labour force in low-productivity activities, they have correspondingly greater scope for increasing the economy-wide labour productivity through labour transfers.

[8] For details on the data and their sources, see Ghose (2001; forthcoming). A full list of the 96 countries included in our sample is provided in Appendix 3.1.

A good deal of research effort has been devoted to testing empirically the convergence hypothesis. The basic result of this research is that the empirical evidence rejects the hypothesis.[9] The observed tendency has been toward divergence of per capita incomes; *inter-country* inequality has shown a persistent tendency to rise. However, in certain periods, it is possible to identify the existence of so-called "convergence clubs", i.e., small groups of countries that show a tendency toward convergence. The globalization of 1870–1913 spawned a "convergence club" that had the countries of Western Europe and the New World as members. The post-war period of economic integration (1950–73) witnessed the catching-up of Southern European countries and Japan with Western Europe and the United States.

As we shall see below, our results for the period 1981–97 identify very similar tendencies. Before discussing these results, however, it is appropriate to note some possible *a priori* reasons as to why the prediction of standard economic theory failed to materialize. First, the process of technological change can be such that there always remains a substantial technology gap between more developed and less developed economies. By the time less developed countries begin to use an established technology, more developed countries could conceivably move to a new one. Second, in the use of any particular technology, there usually is considerable scope for "learning by doing". For this reason, capital productivity need not be higher, and could even be lower, in less developed economies, at least for a certain period of time.

Equivalent rates of investment, therefore, need not produce higher growth in less developed economies. In addition, the employment intensity of the relatively high-productivity sectors in less developed economies tends to be low precisely because borrowed technologies are used. The process of labour transfer from low-productivity to high-productivity sectors also tends to be rather slow as a consequence. Thus productivity gains from intersectoral labour transfers are not necessarily higher in less developed than in more developed countries.

We can now discuss the results of our own empirical analysis. Figure 3.1 plots the average annual rate of growth of per capita GDP during 1981–97 against the initial level of per capita GDP (measured in "purchasing power parity", or PPP dollars, to make them comparable across countries). Given that the initial level of per capita GDP is an indicator of the initial level of development, figure 3.1 tells us that the rate of growth of per capita GDP in fact tended to be slower for less developed economies. The implication is that *inter-country* inequality increased.

[9] There is some evidence of what is called "conditional convergence". For similar rates of saving/investment, stocks of human capital and rates of population growth, poorer countries are found to achieve higher growth than richer countries. Not surprisingly, however, poorer countries tend to have lower saving/investment rates, lower stocks of human capital and higher rates of population growth so that convergence is not observed in reality.

Figure 3.1 Convergence/divergence, 96 economies, 1981–97

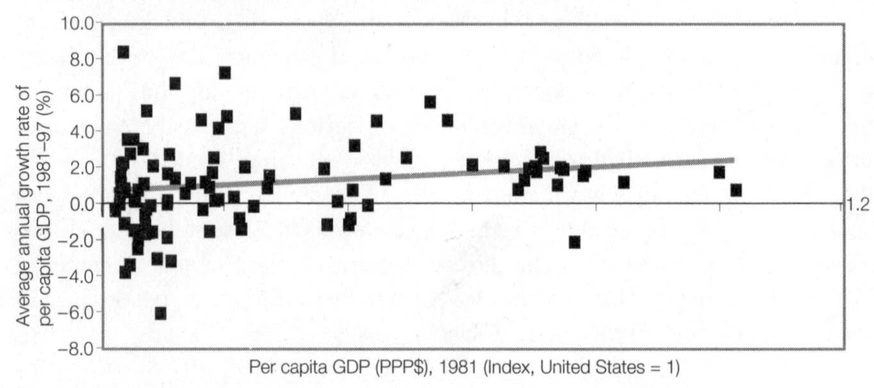

Note: Average annual growth rates refer to per capita GDP in constant local currency unit.
Source: Ghose (2001).

Figure 3.2 Inter-country inequality, 96 economies, 1981–97

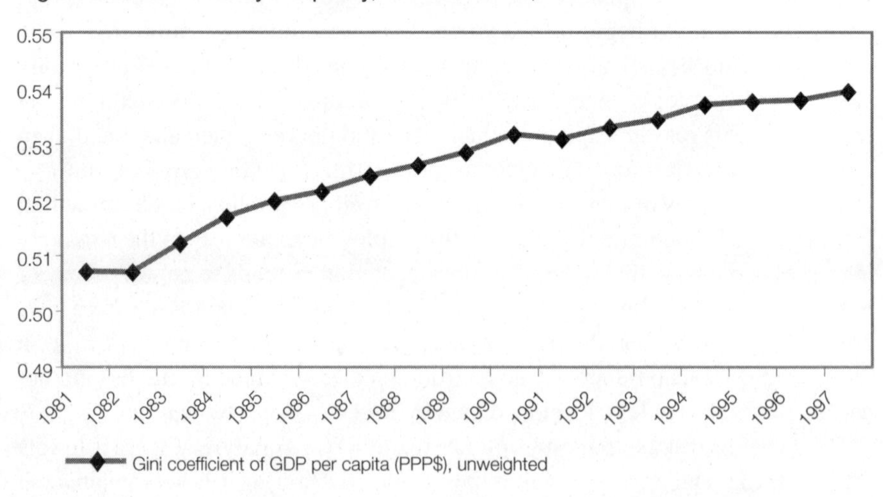

Source: Ghose (2001).

Using a well-known measure of inequality – the Gini coefficient – can show this more explicitly. The Gini coefficient measures the distance of the actual distribution from a hypothetical, wholly equal distribution (when the value of the coefficient is zero), so that a higher value of the coefficient indicates a higher degree of inequality. The values shown in figure 3.2 are estimated by treating each country as an individual; they are measures of *inter-country* inequality of per capita GDP (measured in PPP dollars). The figure shows that *inter-country* inequality rose steadily during the period. Recalling our earlier observations, we can conclude that globalization has not changed the long-term tendency of *inter-country* inequality to rise.

International inequality, 1981–97

The Gini coefficient can also be used to study the trend in *international* inequality. But now we estimate the values of this coefficient by treating each person in a country as an individual with an income that equals the per capita GDP of that country. The estimated values are shown in figure 3.3. It is clear that *international* inequality declined steadily during the period. We know from other studies that, over a long period (1820–1979), *international* inequality rose in some sub-periods and remained stable in others.[10] The declining international inequality during 1981–97, therefore, is something new; it represents a break in the long-term trend.[11]

What explains the decline of international inequality in a period when *inter-country* inequality was rising? Given the nature of definitional differences between the two measures of inequality, the explanation suggests itself: there exists a "convergence club", which includes developing countries that account for a majority of the population of the developing world. Hence an effort is made to identify the members of the convergence club and the result is shown in figure 3.4. The figure shows that a sizeable number of low-income countries recorded significantly higher growth of per capita GDP than the rich, industrialized countries. Of the 37 economies (which, in 1997, accounted for 72 per cent of the total population of our sample countries and 60 per cent of world population) represented in figure 3.4, 17 are developing economies (which, in 1997, accounted for 67 per cent of the total population of the developing countries included in our sample and 62 per cent of the population of the developing world).[12] Of these 17 developing economies, ten are from the Asia-Pacific region, and five of these ten are low-income countries with large populations. In 1997, these five countries (China, India, Indonesia, Pakistan and Thailand) accounted for 93 per cent of the total population of the 17 developing countries

---

[10] See Berry, Bourguignon and Morrisson (1983); Bourguignon and Morrisson (2002); and Schultz (1998).

[11] Sala-i-Martin (2002) shows that the inequality of world *income distribution* fluctuated around a mean in the 1970s but declined steadily between 1980 and 1998. This is rather reassuring as it is consistent with our result and confirms that the *international* inequality and the inequality of world *income distribution* generally move together.

[12] The 37 economies are: Australia, Austria, Belgium, Botswana, Canada, Chile, China, Denmark, Finland, France, Greece, Hong Kong (China), India, Indonesia, Ireland, Israel, Italy, Japan, Republic of Korea, Lesotho, Malaysia, Mauritius, Netherlands, New Zealand, Norway, Pakistan, Portugal, Singapore, Spain, Sri Lanka, Swaziland, Sweden, Switzerland, Thailand, Turkey, United Kingdom and United States. It should be noted that Germany and Taiwan (China) would have been found to belong to the "convergence club", had they been included in our sample of countries.

Figure 3.3 International inequality, 96 economies, 1981–97

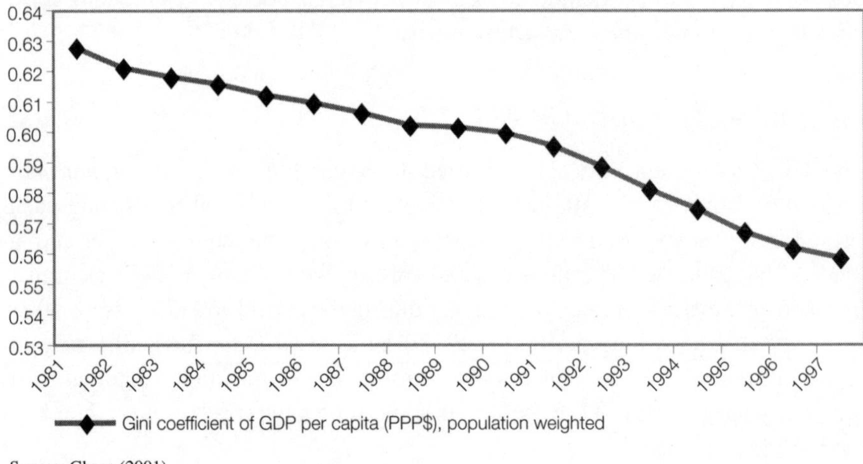

Source: Ghose (2001).

Figure 3.4 The "convergence club", 37 economies, 1981–97

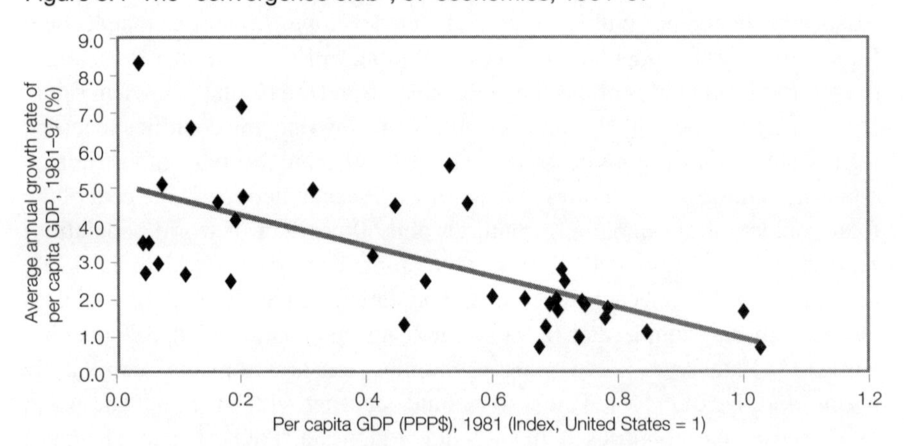

Note: Average annual growth rates refer to per capita GDP in constant local currency unit.

Source: Ghose (2001).

in the convergence club, 63 per cent of the total population of the 76 developing countries included in our sample, and 58 per cent of the total population of the developing world. It is clear, then, that the declining *international* inequality reflected an underlying process of catching-up by a small number of populous countries from Asia, which account for a majority of the population residing in the developing world.

Three remarks are in order. First, this is the first time in history that a number of populous developing countries seem to be catching up with the industrialized world and this clearly is a welcome development. Of all the globalization episodes, the current process is in fact the most inclusive. Second, it is a notable fact that not all successfully integrating developing countries are in the convergence club. This can be seen from a comparison of the list of manufactures-exporting developing countries identified in Chapter 2 (Appendix 2.1) and the list of developing countries in the convergence club identified here (note 9). However, it is also worth noting that all but four of the developing countries that belong to the convergence club are also successful exporters of manufactures.[13] Third, the analysis highlights the problem of global exclusion once again. A majority of the developing countries are falling behind rather than catching up. It is true that they account for a minority of the population of the developing world. It is also true that not all the excluded countries are low-income countries. Nevertheless, the falling-behind of so many less developed countries is certainly not a sign of health for the emerging global economy. And, most worryingly, virtually all the least developed countries are among the excluded.[14]

Trade liberalization and global income inequality

Did the widespread trade liberalization, which occurred during 1981–97, play a role in bringing about the observed trends in *inter-country* and *international* inequalities? Clearly, trade liberalization could conceivably affect these inequalities in so far as it could have differential impact on the pace of economic growth of individual countries. But the effect of trade liberalization on economic growth is not direct. In the first instance, trade liberalization is expected to affect trade performance of countries. Trade performance, in turn, is expected to affect economic growth. We therefore need to find answers to the two following questions. First, how did trade liberalization affect trade performance of countries? Second, did trade performance affect economic growth of countries? Once we know the answers, we can study the patterns of variation in trade performance across countries to see whether and how trade liberalization affected global income inequality.

We have already seen (in Chapter 2) that virtually all countries liberalized trade during the period under study. The process started in the early 1980s and

[13] The four countries are Botswana, Chile, Lesotho and Swaziland. The prosperity of the three small countries – Botswana, Lesotho and Swaziland – is based on exports of diamonds. Chile is still largely dependent on exports of primary commodities, but its manufactured exports have grown at an impressive rate.

[14] The United Nations classifies 49 countries as "least developed". These are listed in Appendix 3.1. Our sample of 96 countries includes 24 of these 49 least developed countries.

continued throughout the period, though the period between the mid-1980s and the early 1990s was the most significant liberalization period. Of course, the initial degree of openness as well as the extent of liberalization varied widely across countries. But the fact remains that the degree of openness increased for all countries. To this extent we can plausibly suppose that the observed changes in trade performance of countries during the period are, in large part, the result of trade liberalization.

How do we measure change in trade performance? The widely accepted measure is the change in trade–GDP ratio. An increase (decrease) in this ratio is taken to indicate an improvement (deterioration) in trade performance. Our data set allows us to estimate the change in trade–GDP ratio for 95 countries and the results are presented in table 3.1. The basic impression that emerges is that the effect of trade liberalization on trade performance has been extremely varied across countries. At one end of the spectrum, 13 countries suffered a serious deterioration in trade performance. At the other end, 25 countries achieved quite dramatic improvement in their trade performance. Trade liberalization has not been good for trade in all cases.

This should not surprise anyone. The effect of trade liberalization on trade performance is mediated by a host of other factors and hence cannot be uniform across countries. For example, conditions of the global market in products that a particular country exports or can export clearly matter. As noted in Chapter 2, there is evidence to show that the global demand for primary commodities was stagnant for much of the period under review. Under such circumstances, trade liberalization could not possibly have helped the exporters of primary commodities to improve their trade performance. Indeed, the trade performance of these countries might have worsened even in the absence of trade liberalization. On the other hand, had the global demand for primary commodities grown rapidly, the

Table 3.1 Variation in trade performance, 1981–97

Average annual rate of change (%) in trade–GDP ratio, 1981–97	Number of countries (% of sample)
Less than –2.01	2 (2.2)
–2.0 to –1.01	11 (11.6)
–1.0 to 0.0	18 (18.9)
0.01 to 1.0	23 (24.2)
1.01 to 2.0	16 (16.8)
2.01 to 3.0	11 (11.6)
Greater than 3.0	14 (14.7)
All	95 (100)

Source: Derived from Ghose (2001), Appendix table 2.

Figure 3.5 Trade performance and economic growth, 95 economies

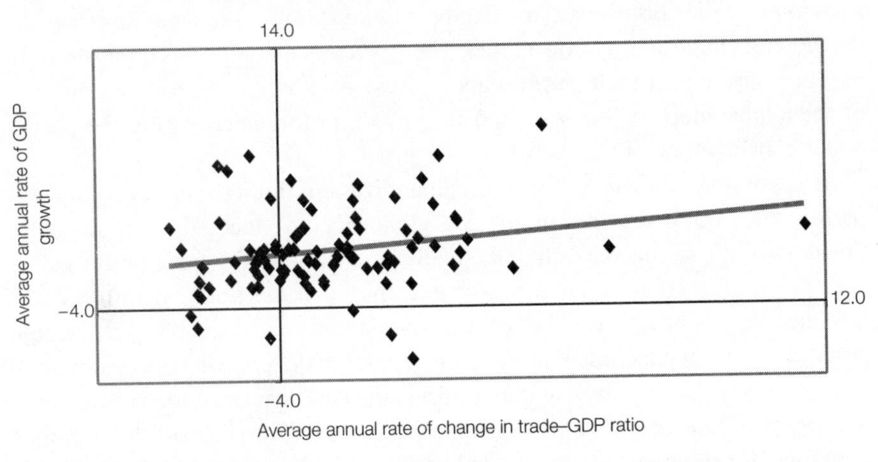

Source: Ghose (2001).

exporters of primary commodities would probably have improved their trade performance even without trade liberalization, though trade liberalization would certainly have added to the gains.

How did trade performance affect economic growth? Figure 3.5 plots, for 95 countries, the average annual rate of GDP growth against the average annual rate of change in trade–GDP ratio. It shows that the two variables were positively related. The countries that achieved improvement in trade performance also achieved higher growth; correspondingly, the countries that suffered deterioration in trade performance also achieved poor growth. Moreover, the larger the improvement (deterioration) in trade performance, the better (worse) was the growth performance.

It does seem, therefore, that improved trade performance had a positive impact on growth. However, this finding cannot be accepted as valid without further investigation. For trade performance is not the only factor that influences growth performance. It is possible that when other factors contributing to economic growth are taken into account, the effect of trade performance will disappear. To rule out this possibility, we have carried out some appropriate econometric exercises.[15] The detailed results are not reported here, but they show the positive relationship between the change in trade performance and the rate of GDP growth to be quite robust. The relationship survives (in an econometrically meaningful sense) even after the contribution

[15] See Ghose (2002).

of other factors to GDP growth has been taken into account and even when subsamples of countries (for example, only low- and medium-income developing countries) are considered. Thus the evidence suggests quite strongly that the variation in trade performance across countries was an important part of the explanation for the variation in growth performance during the period under consideration. Trade was good for growth.

It is possible, therefore, that trade liberalization, through its effect on trade performance, played a role in altering global income inequality. To consider this possibility, we need to study the patterns of variation in trade performance across countries. If it is the case, for example, that the trade performance of low-income countries was systematically poorer than that of high-income countries, we can conclude that trade liberalization did contribute to the growth of *inter-country* inequality. Similarly, if it is the case that the trade performance of more populous countries was systematically superior to that of less populous countries, we can conclude that trade liberalization did contribute to the decline of *international* inequality.

Figure 3.6 shows that the trade performance of low-income countries was in fact generally better than that of high-income countries. It certainly cannot be said that the effect of trade liberalization on economic growth was systematically more adverse for low-income countries. And this means that trade liberalization played no significant role in increasing *inter-country* inequality.

On the other hand, as table 3.2 shows, there is some evidence to suggest that the trade performance of more populous countries tended to be superior to that

Figure 3.6 Trade performance and level of development, 95 economies

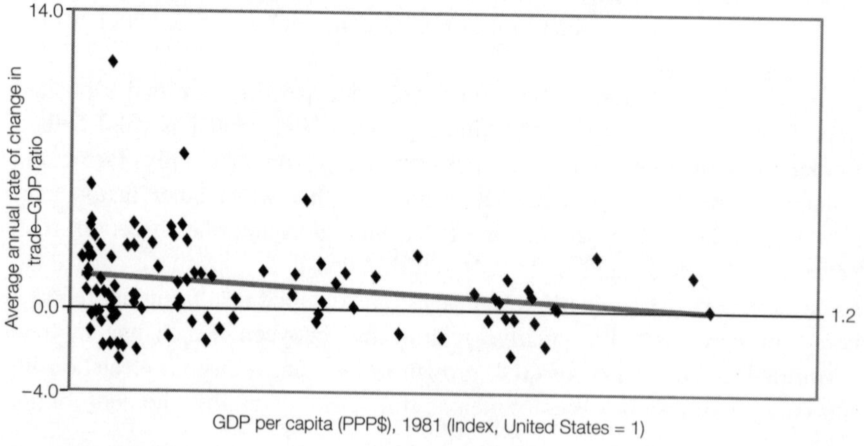

14.0
Average annual rate of change in trade–GDP ratio
0.0
−4.0
1.2
GDP per capita (PPP$), 1981 (Index, United States = 1)

Source: Ghose (2001).

Table 3.2 Patterns of variation in trade–GDP ratio

Population in 1981	Total number of countries	Number of countries for which the trade–GDP ratio declined (% of sample)
Less than 10 million	58	22 (37.9)
10–35 million	17	5 (29.4)
More than 35 million	20	4 (20.0)
All	95	31 (32.6)

Source: Derived from Ghose (2001), Appendix table 2.

of less populous countries. Why this was so is a question that need not detain us here. The fact that it was so means that the effect of trade liberalization on economic growth tended to be more favourable for more populous countries. And this means that trade liberalization contributed to the decline in *international* inequality.

Factually, therefore, there is no basis for arguing that globalization has increased global income inequality. In fact, it is more reasonable to say that globalization has reduced this inequality. Why, then, has *inter-country* inequality increased? The answer seems to lie in the pattern of demographic change across countries. Figure 3.7 shows that there was a strong inverse relationship between the rate of population growth and the initial per capita GDP; population growth tended to be faster in poorer countries. Thus, though GDP growth was certainly no slower in poorer countries, per capita GDP growth was substantially slower.

Figure 3.7 Demographic change and income, 96 economies

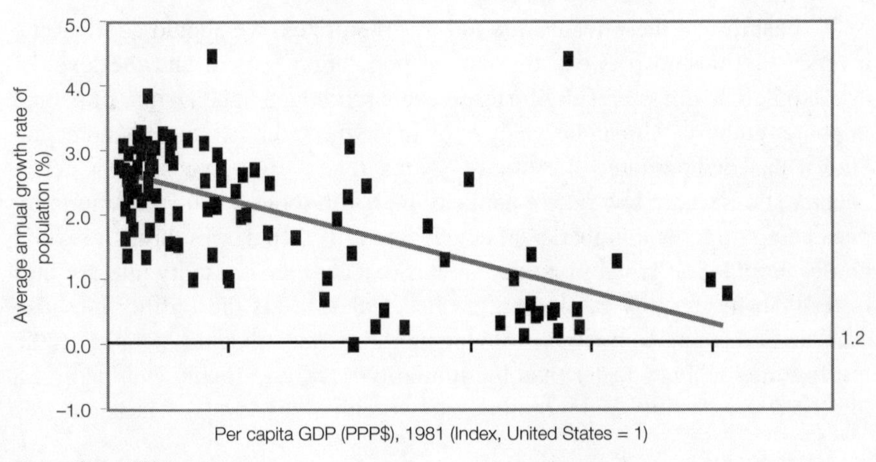

Source: Ghose (2001).

Figure 3.8 Demographic change and international inequality, 1981–97

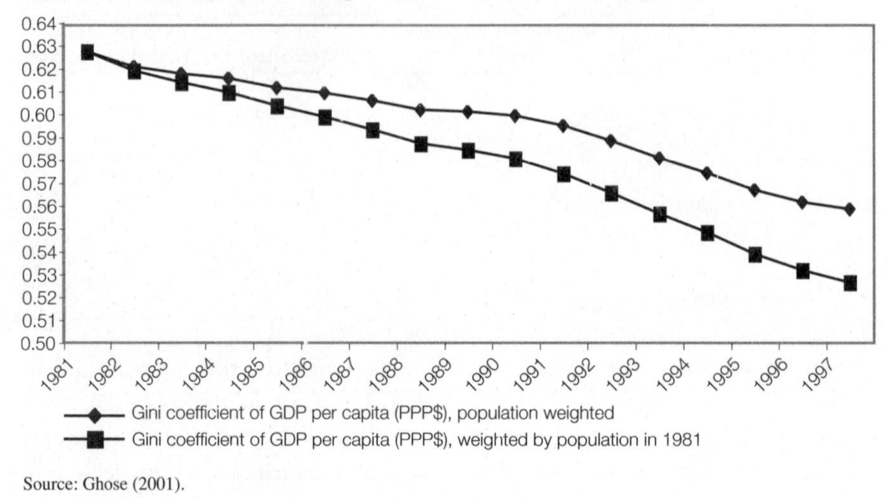

Source: Ghose (2001).

In fact, the pattern of demographic change across countries also had the effect of slowing down the decline in *international* inequality. This is clear from figure 3.8. The upper curve is the same as that shown in figure 3.3. The lower curve shows the hypothetical trajectory that would have been observed had the distribution of world population across countries remained the same as that found in 1981 (that is, had the rate of population growth during 1981–97 been the same for all countries). What figure 3.8 shows is that the decline in *international* inequality would have been sharper but for the differential rates of population growth across countries.

To ensure that these results are not misinterpreted, we should add that the inverse relationship between the rate of population growth and the level of development is not the result of irresponsible reproductive behaviour of people in poorer countries. It can be easily explained with reference to a phenomenon known as "demographic transition".[16] This refers to a process in which a country starts with a low rate of population growth (both fertility and mortality rates being high) as it embarks on development. It then passes through several phases. Population growth first accelerates (because the mortality rate declines faster than the fertility rate), then reaches a plateau (as the fertility rate also declines and begins to catch up with the mortality rate), then decelerates (as the fertility rate declines faster than the mortality rate), and finally stabilizes at a low rate (both fertility and mortality rates reaching low levels). These patterns

[16] See Birdsall (1988) and Kelley (1988) for discussions of the theory of demographic transition.

have been observed in all countries. But because different countries embarked on development at different points of time in history, they are in different phases of demographic transition at any given point of time. The inverse relationship between the rate of population growth and the level of development, observed across countries, simply reflects the fact that poorer countries have also been late starters on the path to development.

Conclusions

The widespread perception that globalization is increasing global income inequality does not seem to have a secure foundation in empirical reality. The assertion that global income inequality has been rising in recent years is correct only if we define global income inequality as *inter-country* inequality. But then we must also recognize that this inequality has been rising for a long time and is not a special feature of the last two decades of the twentieth century. More importantly, because of the enormous variation between countries in terms of population size, *inter-country* inequality is not a good measure of global income inequality. A more appropriate measure is that of *international* inequality. When this measure is used, we observe a decline in global income inequality since the early 1980s. And this actually is a novel feature of the global economy. The underlying fact is that a number of populous low-income countries, accounting for a majority of the population residing in the developing world, achieved a faster growth of per capita GDP than the high-income industrialized countries.

Moreover, contrary to popular perception, globalization has actually had a favourable rather than adverse effect on global income inequality. Our analysis of the available empirical evidence shows that trade liberalization helped reduce *international* inequality but had no significant effect on *inter-country* inequality. In essence, the growth of *inter-country* inequality is explained by the pattern of demographic change across countries, which reflects the fact that different countries are in different phases of demographic transition.

In fact, the problem that should cause deep concern is not that of global inequality; it is that of global exclusion, of the least developed countries in particular.

Appendix 3.1

List of countries[17]

The list of 96 countries used for empirical analysis in this chapter is as follows.

ID: Australia, Austria, Belgium, Canada, Denmark, Finland, France, Greece, Ireland, Italy, Japan, Netherlands, New Zealand, Norway, Portugal, Spain, Sweden, Switzerland, United Kingdom, United States (20)

ME: Argentina, Bangladesh, Brazil, China, Egypt, Hong Kong (China), India, Indonesia, Israel, Korea (Republic), Malaysia, Mauritius, Mexico, Morocco, Pakistan, Philippines, Singapore, South Africa, Sri Lanka, Thailand, Tunisia, Turkey (22)

PE: Algeria, Cameroon, Ecuador, Gabon, Nigeria, Saudi Arabia, Venezuela (7)

DC: Benin, *Botswana*, Burkina Faso, Burundi, Central African Republic, Chad, Chile, Colombia, Congo (Republic), Congo (Democratic Republic), Costa Rica, Côte d'Ivoire, Dominican Republic, El Salvador, Ethiopia, Fiji, Gambia, Ghana, Guatemala, Haiti, Honduras, Jamaica, Jordan, Kenya, *Lesotho*, Madagascar, Malawi, Mali, Mauritania, Mongolia, Mozambique, *Namibia*, Nepal, Niger, Paraguay, Peru, Rwanda, Senegal, Sierra Leone, Sudan, *Swaziland*, Syrian Arab Republic, Togo, Trinidad and Tobago, Uruguay, Zambia, Zimbabwe (47)

Countries whose names are italicized do not appear in the list in Appendix 2.1.

The least developed countries, as defined by the United Nations, are as follows.

Afghanistan, Angola, Bangladesh, Benin, Bhutan, Burkina Faso, Burundi, Cambodia, Cape Verde, Central African Republic, Chad, Comoros, Congo (Democratic Republic), Djibouti, Equatorial Guinea, Eritrea, Ethiopia, Gambia, Guinea, Guinea-Bissau, Haiti, Kiribati, Lao People's Democratic Republic, Lesotho, Liberia, Madagascar, Malawi, Maldives, Mali, Mauritania, Mozambique, Myanmar, Nepal, Niger, Rwanda, Samoa, São Tomé and Principe, Senegal, Sierra Leone, Solomon Islands, Somalia, Sudan, Togo, Tuvalu, Tanzania (United Republic), Uganda, Vanuatu, Yemen and Zambia (49)

[17] This list includes territories, areas and regions.

APPENDIX 3.2

Percentage distribution of population by the inequality trend in countries of residence

	Growing inequality	Stable inequality	Decreasing inequality	No identifiable trend
Industrialized countries	71.8	1.2	27.0	0.0
Eastern Europe	98.1	0.0	0.0	1.9
Former Soviet Union	100.0	0.0	0.0	0.0
Latin America	83.8	0.0	11.4	4.8
South Asia and Middle East	1.4	70.2	14.4	14.0
East Asia	79.4	4.4	16.1	0.1
Africa	31.6	11.9	7.7	48.8
World	56.6	22.1	15.6	5.7

Source: ECLAC (2002), p. 82, table 3.4.

TRADE, JOBS AND WAGES 4

Introduction

The effect of the growth of international trade on employment and wages in national economies has been and remains a subject of deep concern and serious controversy. In industrialized countries, the growth of trade with low-income developing countries is often held responsible for the growth of inequalities, in terms of both employment prospects and wage earnings, between high-skilled and low-skilled workers. In developing countries, growing trade-openness is also viewed with a good deal of suspicion. It is alleged to be destroying "good" jobs in previously protected sectors while generating "bad" jobs in new "sweatshops" producing for export. Such developments, moreover, are sometimes thought to be aggravating the problem of poverty. Thus the expansion of world trade, according to these views, has brought little benefit to workers; its consequences for jobs and incomes have allegedly been adverse everywhere.

Yet none of this is empirically well established and, for economists, the issue of linkage between trade and labour market developments remains very much open. In the large literature that exists on industrialized countries, there is consensus that inequalities between high-skilled and low-skilled workers have indeed been rising since the early 1980s. But there is no agreement on the idea that this trend is explained by the growth of trade with low-income developing countries. In fact, to most economists, a more plausible explanation for the trend appears to be technological change, which has been skill biased (requiring the use of proportionately more skilled labour). In the context of developing countries, serious empirical investigations into the issues have been rare; indeed, it is quite striking how the debate on the subject has been dominated by issues of relevance to industrialized countries alone. The few studies on developing countries that do exist show the labour market effects of trade to have been somewhat varied across countries.

In this chapter, we take a fresh look at the effects of expansion of world trade on employment and wages in both industrialized and developing countries. We first examine what economic theory leads us to expect these effects to be. We then report the results of recent ILO research on the issues and place them in the context of the results already available from the literature.[1]

There are two premises for the analysis presented in this chapter. First, as already noted in Chapter 2, the novel feature of trade expansion since the mid-1980s has been the rapid growth of two-way trade in manufactures between industrialized countries and a group of developing countries. As such, in both types of countries we should expect to observe the most direct effects of trade on employment and wages in manufacturing industries. Indeed, we have already seen that a process of global redistribution of manufacturing employment has been under way. Our focus in this chapter, therefore, is on the effects of trade on employment and wages in manufacturing industries. The economy-wide effects (which we do not discuss) depend on the structural characteristics of the economy in question. At a general level, it is useful to bear the following points in mind. In many of the industrialized countries, the share of manufacturing industries in total employment was on the decline prior to the globalization period; a process of deindustrialization had been under way since the early 1970s. Thus the economy-wide trends in employment and wages are influenced more by the trends in services than by those in manufacturing. For this reason, the effects of trade on economy-wide employment and wages are not expected to be particularly significant even if they are significant for employment and wages in manufacturing. In developing countries, in contrast, transfer of labour from agriculture (and other traditional activities) into modern manufacturing is the key to economic transformation. Employment and wages in manufacturing industries, therefore, are critical determinants of economy-wide conditions of employment and labour incomes. As such, the effects of trade on employment and wages in manufacturing industries are of crucial significance.

Second, we have also seen (in Chapters 2 and 3) that only a small number of developing countries (though they account for a majority of the population of the developing world) have actually emerged as successful exporters of manufactures to industrialized countries. It is in the manufacturing industries of these countries that we should expect to observe the most direct employment and wage effects of trade. In this chapter, therefore, we confine attention to industrialized countries on the one hand and the manufactures-exporting developing countries on the other. For the globally excluded developing

[1] Under an ILO research project on globalization and employment, six detailed case studies have been carried out. These are: Landesmann et al. (2002), Woo and Ren (2002), Goldar (2002), Rasiah (2002), Palma (2002) and Vernengo (2002). The studies provide both fresh empirical analyses and good reviews of the relevant literature.

countries, there has been little change in the nature of trade; they still export primary commodities and import manufactures, as they have always done. In the case of these countries, the effects of trade on employment and wages arise from movements in international prices of primary commodities and not from a global restructuring of production. In general, trade liberalization has not helped these countries to increase export revenues, as international prices of primary commodities have been declining. Indeed, trade liberalization has sometimes hurt them, as when it has prematurely exposed nascent manufacturing industries to international competition or when it has opened the door to imports of highly subsidized agricultural products from industrialized countries.[2] On the whole, however, it is contraction and not expansion of trade that has caused economic difficulties and impoverishment of population in these countries.

What does economic theory tell us?

The basic analytical framework

Most of the current ideas about the effect of trade on jobs and wages can be derived from a simple version of the mainstream trade theory that considers two countries (North and South), two factors (skilled and unskilled labour) and two products (skill-intensive and unskilled-labour-intensive manufactures).[3] By assumption, both North (industrialized countries) and South (developing countries) have access to similar technologies, capital is fully mobile and labour is fully immobile across national frontiers. The two countries, therefore, differ only in terms of the skill composition of the labour force. North has a higher proportion of skilled workers in its labour force and hence has a potential comparative advantage in the production of the skill-intensive manufactured good. South, with its relatively abundant supply of unskilled workers, has a potential comparative advantage in the production of the unskilled-labour-intensive manufactured good.

Under autarky, both goods are produced in each country in proportions determined by the composition of domestic demand, and the labour force in each country is fully employed to produce them. The relative prices and wages are determined by the country-specific labour supply conditions; thus the relative wage of skilled labour and the relative price of the skill-intensive good are higher in the South. As trade barriers are lowered and the two countries export to and

[2] See Oxfam (2002), Ch. 6, for a detailed discussion.

[3] For an elaborate exposition, see Wood (1994).

import from each other, the relative price of the unskilled-labour-intensive good falls in the North (because it can be imported from the South at a cheaper price) and the relative price of the skill-intensive good falls in the South (because it can be imported from the North at a cheaper price). Hence, in the North, the production of the skill-intensive good (which is now exported to the South) expands and the production of the unskilled-labour-intensive good (which is now imported from the South) contracts; the opposite happens in the South.

The labour market effects of these changes are fairly easy to work out. In the North, the demand for skilled labour rises and that for unskilled labour falls. Thus the real wage of skilled labour rises and that of unskilled labour falls, so that the wage gap between skilled and unskilled labour rises.[4] In the South, the demand for unskilled labour rises and that for skilled labour falls. Thus the real wage of unskilled labour rises and that of skilled labour falls, so that the wage gap between skilled and unskilled labour falls.[5]

The predictions of the mainstream trade theory can be summed up as follows. Trade (between industrialized and developing countries) adversely affects unskilled labour in industrialized countries but benefits unskilled labour in developing countries. On the other hand, it adversely affects skilled labour in developing countries and benefits skilled labour in industrialized countries. In consequence, inequalities between skilled and unskilled labour increase in industrialized countries and decline in developing countries. What happens to total employment depends on labour market regulations and institutions. If wage adjustments are difficult, total employment falls. With smooth wage adjustments, there is no change in total employment; the only change is in the allocation of labour between industries.

These predictions, it must be emphasized, hold only when trade occurs in competing products (that is, products which are or could be produced in both trading countries). They would not hold, for example, when trade occurs between two countries, one of which is capable of producing only coffee and sugar and the other is capable of producing only televisions and watches. The relevance of the analytical framework outlined above depends critically on the assumption that the trading economies are in principle capable of producing the full set of traded goods. This is why the framework is appropriate for analysis of two-way trade in manufactures (which, in principle, could be produced anywhere).

[4] As the real wage of unskilled labour falls, technology adjusts so that the surplus unskilled labour is re-employed in the production of the skill-intensive good (which becomes somewhat less skill-intensive in the process). If labour market regulations and institutions are such as to prevent a fall in the real wage, there is some unemployment of unskilled labour.

[5] Once again, as the real wage of skilled labour falls, technology adjusts so that the surplus skilled labour is re-employed in the production of the unskilled-labour-intensive good (which becomes somewhat less unskilled-labour-intensive in the process). If the real wage cannot adjust downward, there is some unemployment of skilled labour.

This point needs to be emphasized as it is all too often forgotten or ignored, which introduces serious distortions into analysis of North–South trade. When Switzerland trades electric locomotives for cocoa with Côte d'Ivoire, comparative advantage cannot be the reason, for Switzerland is not in a position to produce cocoa at any cost. A substantial number of primary products, exported by developing countries, cannot in fact be produced in the industrialized countries that import them. Trade in such cases is not about acquiring access to lower-cost products but about acquiring access to previously unavailable products. In this kind of trade, the relative prices of the traded goods do not depend on relative factor endowments of the trading countries; they are determined by the conditions of demand and supply in the world market. The consequences of trade for employment and labour incomes depend on how relative prices move and not on how production is restructured. The theory of comparative advantage cannot be used to analyse these consequences.

A necessary dose of realism

The basic framework outlined above is based on several assumptions that do not correspond to reality. In the real world, for example, all countries do not have access to the same technologies, capital is not fully mobile across national frontiers and labour is not fully immobile. Nevertheless, we can accept some of these simplifying abstractions as reasonable approximations of reality. Both technologies and capital, for example, move fairly easily across national frontiers in today's world. And the prevailing restrictions on international labour mobility are rather severe.[6] Given our focus on the labour market effects of trade, however, it is vitally important to consider the consequences of abandoning one particular assumption, that of full employment of labour in both North and South under autarky. Full employment is a reasonable assumption for industrialized countries, but it is certainly inappropriate for developing countries.

As a matter of fact, most developing countries have dualistic labour markets and substantial stocks of surplus unskilled labour. A stylized account of labour market conditions in a typical developing country is as follows. A regulated sector (defined here to mean the sector where government regulations and collective bargaining institutions play a critical role in determining wages and conditions of work),[7] which under autarky produces skill-intensive goods,

[6] The nature of international labour mobility is examined in some detail in Chapter 5 below.

[7] To avoid confusion, we should emphasize that what we call the regulated sector is not the same as what is known as the formal sector, or formal economy; by implication, the non-regulated sector is not equivalent to the informal economy. The formal economy is usually defined with reference to the enterprise size and/or the degree of capital use. We define the regulated sector with reference to the role of government regulations and collective bargaining institutions (for example, trade unions).

employs the entire stock of skilled labour but only a small part of the stock of unskilled labour. Most of the unskilled workers are engaged in a wide variety of activities (some with very low productivity), including regular wage employment in unskilled-labour-intensive manufacturing enterprises, outside the regulated sector. Because there is no universal social security system, unskilled workers generally cannot afford to be unemployed and are forced to engage in virtually any activity with a positive productivity (however low). Thus, though there usually is little open unemployment, many apparently employed unskilled workers are not in fact employed in any meaningful sense; even apparent full employment conceals a substantial stock of surplus unskilled labour. Many unskilled workers seek wage employment on a daily basis, and many others are in low-productivity self-employment; these are the labour market features that underlie the widespread absolute poverty. Dualism is manifest in the fact that the unskilled workers employed in the regulated sector earn a much higher wage (and enjoy much better conditions of work) than those outside it (where forces of demand and supply hold sway).

Under these conditions, a rise in the demand for unskilled labour, resulting from a lowering of trade barriers, need not necessarily increase its real wage. So long as there is a stock of surplus unskilled labour (in the sense indicated above), manufacturing enterprises, whether inside or outside the regulated sector, have no problem in expanding employment at the ruling wage rates. As unskilled-labour-intensive manufacturing occurs mostly outside the regulated sector, trade-induced employment expansion also occurs mostly outside the regulated sector. Skill-intensive manufacturing industries in the regulated sector are transformed into import-competing industries as trade openness replaces autarky. As a result, the employment of unskilled workers in the regulated sector may well decline (though job protection systems often make this a very slow process), as the sector may shrink in the face of import competition. Thus even when there is no change in wages of unskilled workers in any particular activity, the average real wage of unskilled labour in manufacturing industries as a whole could still fall because of a decline in the proportion of unskilled workers employed in the regulated sector.

On the other hand, a fall in the demand for skilled labour need not lead either to a fall in employment or to a fall in the real wage of skilled labour. In the regulated sector, where virtually the entire skilled labour force is employed, fairly strict job protection systems are usually in place and downward flexibility of wages is rare. Hence neither employment nor wages of skilled labour may fall. In fact, because of the importance of government regulations and collective bargaining, it is even possible for the real wage of skilled labour to rise.

In short, in the context of developing countries, we should expect the main effect of trade to be a rise in the employment of unskilled labour. Theory predicts that the intensity of manufacturing production by unskilled labour would rise. And, given dualistic labour markets, unskilled workers outside the regulated sector can be expected to be the main beneficiaries. But average real wages and wage inequality could move in an unpredictable manner, so long as the stock of surplus unskilled labour remains sizeable and government regulations and collective bargaining institutions govern the conditions of employment of skilled labour.

It needs to be emphasized, however, that expansion of employment of unskilled labour in manufacturing industries, even outside the regulated sector, is almost always poverty reducing. The reason is that wage-earnings from regular jobs, whether inside or outside the regulated sector, are generally above the poverty line. Absolute poverty in developing countries is largely confined to the casual wage-labourers and the self-employed with a poor asset base. Thus growth (decline) of poverty is associated with the expansion (contraction) of the size of these categories of workers. Trade-induced industrial restructuring reduces poverty so long as it results in the growth of regular, full-time jobs for unskilled workers. It should also be clear that even a declining average real wage of unskilled labour in manufacturing industries does not necessarily indicate growth of poverty, for this often results from a change in the composition of employment and not from a fall in the ruling real wage rates. There has been much confusion on these points in the literature, where any evidence that jobs in export industries are of lower quality than those in the regulated sector or that there is a decline in the average real wage of unskilled labour is unhesitatingly interpreted to mean rising poverty.

The empirical evidence

Trade and the pattern of specialization

For the predictions of the mainstream trade theory examined in this chapter to be relevant in practice, it must be true that trade between industrialized and developing countries involves specialization of the former in skill-intensive manufactures and specialization of the latter in unskilled-labour-intensive manufactures. So we need to start by asking if this proposition is supported by evidence.

One kind of evidence is presented in table 4.1. This shows the composition of manufactured exports (to all destinations) and imports (from all sources) of two groups of countries – industrialized (ID) countries and manufactures-

Table 4.1 Manufactured trade by technology category, various years

	Structure of manufactured exports (%)			Structure of manufactured imports (%)		
	1980–82	1989–91	1996–98	1980–82	1989–91	1996–98
ID countries						
HT	14.3	18.6	21.8	14.3	18.6	22.5
MHT	52.3	51.7	50.6	47.8	46.5	44.8
MLT	19.8	15.7	14.3	19.5	16.7	15.4
LT	10.7	10.6	9.7	15.3	14.7	13.5
NS	2.9	3.4	3.6	3.1	3.5	3.8
ME countries						
HT	12.8	21.1	28.9	13.9	21.1	26.9
MHT	23.1	24.2	27.2	52.1	46.4	42.1
MLT	26.5	21.1	17.1	20.6	16.0	13.5
LT	35.9	30.4	22.1	10.3	13.2	12.1
NS	1.7	3.2	4.7	3.1	3.3	5.4

Note: The classification scheme used is that of the OECD. Technology categories: HT – high technology; MHT – medium-high technology; MLT – medium-low technology; LT – low technology; NS – not specified.

Source: Ghose and Matsumoto (2002).

exporting (ME) developing countries – in terms of technology content of products.[8] The technology content of a product also indicates its skill intensity; indeed, a ranking of industries by the level of technology closely matches a ranking by skill intensity.[9] Table 4.1 thus shows that industrialized countries do tend to specialize in exports of skill-intensive (or "high-technology" and "medium-high-technology") products, while developing countries tend to specialize in exports of unskilled-labour-intensive (or "low-technology" and "medium-low-technology") products. Though the manufactures-exporting developing countries have been increasing the skill intensity of their exports over time, low-technology and medium-low-technology products still accounted for over 39 per cent of their exports at the end of the 1990s; the corresponding figure for ID countries was 26 per cent. A comparison of the structure of exports with that of imports also brings out the nature of

[8] The classification of industries is that developed by the OECD. It is based on a ranking of industries by the share of research and development (R&D) expenditure in value added. Appendix 4.1 provides the list of classified industries for easy reference.

[9] See Appendix 4.1.

specialization of each group of countries. It is fairly obvious that, for the ID countries, high-technology and medium-high-technology products dominate exports, while low-technology and medium-low-technology products dominate imports. The opposite is true for the ME countries.

However, high-technology exports apparently account for a larger percentage of total exports for ME countries than for ID countries, and this seems contrary to expectation. But much of the high-technology exports from ME countries is in fact the result of outsourcing by transnational corporations (TNCs) based in ID countries. The TNCs are increasingly locating the relatively low-technology component production or assembly operation in developing countries through investment or subcontracting arrangements.[10] Studies have shown that outsourcing-related high-technology exports of developing countries tend to be somewhat more skill-intensive than their domestically generated exports but far less skill-intensive than their high-technology imports.[11] Thus the fact that high-technology exports account for a substantial and growing proportion of manufactured exports from developing countries does not substantially alter the fact that developing countries tend to specialize in unskilled-labour-intensive exports.

Country-level studies confirm this pattern of specialization. A recent ILO study, which analyses the labour market effects of trade in seven industrialized countries over the period 1980–96, shows that while the level of import penetration from developing countries was highest in low-skill industries, the growth of import penetration was fastest in high-skill industries, indicating rapid growth of outsourcing in these industries.[12]

Table 4.2 shows the structure of manufactured exports and imports in terms of technology level for five major ME countries. On the whole, these data confirm what has been observed above: imports are more skill-intensive than exports for all five countries, though the differential is small in the cases of Brazil and Mexico (particularly in the case of Mexico). However, there are some interesting differences among the countries, and these are worth noting. Low-skill-intensive (low-technology and medium-low-technology) products dominate exports from China and India in the way the standard trade theory predicts. In contrast, products of skill-intensive (high-technology and medium-high-technology) industries dominate exports from Brazil, Malaysia and Mexico. It thus appears that while final goods dominate the exports from China and India, outsourced intermediate goods dominate the exports from Brazil, Malaysia and Mexico. This means that

[10] See Lall (2001), and Arndt and Kierzkowski (2001).

[11] See Feenstra and Hanson, 2001.

[12] See Landesmann et al. (2002). The seven countries covered in the study are: France, Germany, Japan, Netherlands, Sweden, United Kingdom and United States.

Table 4.2 Manufactured trade by technology category, selected ME countries, various years

	Structure of manufactured exports (%)			Structure of manufactured imports (%)		
	1980–82	1989–91	1996–98	1980–82	1989–91	1996–98
Brazil						
HT	8.2	7.5	7.1	15.9	17.1	18.4
MHT	46.7	44.4	40.5	63.4	60.3	59.4
MLT	28.0	31.9	35.6	13.4	14.8	14.0
LT	15.9	15.2	15.5	4.0	4.5	5.1
NS	1.2	1.0	1.3	3.3	3.3	3.1
China						
HT	2.7	2.9	3.8	7.8	8.9	11.7
MHT	17.6	16.9	16.6	50.4	48.2	46.9
MLT	18.8	18.1	16.3	26.0	27.6	28.5
LT	58.1	59.3	58.5	13.2	13.1	11.2
NS	2.8	2.8	4.8	2.6	2.2	1.7
India						
HT	2.7	3.0	3.8	13.9	12.9	12.3
MHT	19.6	17.8	18.9	46.2	45.5	45.9
MLT	26.1	29.2	27.9	32.9	35.1	35.6
LT	49.5	47.5	47.4	3.7	3.4	3.1
NS	2.1	2.5	2.0	3.3	3.1	3.1
Malaysia						
HT	55.5	58.0	59.8	17.0	20.5	24.7
MHT	12.3	12.8	13.2	53.3	49.6	46.2
MLT	7.9	7.8	7.6	19.2	19.7	18.8
LT	21.7	19.6	17.3	8.4	8.0	7.8
NS	2.6	1.8	2.1	2.1	2.2	2.5
Mexico						
HT	6.3	13.2	16.6	10.9	11.7	13.4
MHT	59.0	52.8	49.7	61.5	61.0	60.6
MLT	20.0	19.4	19.2	18.8	18.0	15.6
LT	13.2	11.0	10.0	6.2	6.5	6.4
NS	1.5	3.6	4.5	2.6	2.8	4.0

Note: The classification scheme used is that of OECD. See Appendix 4.1. Technology categories: HT – high technology; MHT – medium-high technology; MLT – medium-low technology; LT – low technology; NS – not specified.

Source: Ghose and Matsumoto (2002).

exports from the latter three countries, though less skill-intensive than their imports, are also somewhat more skill-intensive than the exports from China and India. There is also an interesting difference between Malaysia on the one hand and Brazil and Mexico on the other. While outsourcing from Malaysia is overwhelmingly in high-technology industries (those manufacturing office and computing equipment or radio, television and communication equipment, for example), outsourcing from Brazil and Mexico is mainly in medium-high-technology industries (such as motor vehicles, electrical and non-electrical machinery). In other words, outsourcing from Malaysia is in "new" industries, while that from Brazil and Mexico is in "old" capital-intensive industries, industries that were usually nurtured in developing countries under autarkic import substitution regimes. These differences, as we shall see below, are important sources of differences in labour market effects of trade.

Employment and wages in industrialized countries

During the period under analysis – indeed, since the late 1970s – unskilled workers fared poorly in most industrialized countries. In the United States, the real wage of unskilled workers showed a declining trend over a fairly long period. In Western Europe, where labour market institutions constrained downward flexibility of real wages, unemployment grew among the unskilled. Wage inequality between skilled and unskilled workers showed a rising trend in both parts of the world. These economy-wide trends are fairly well documented and uncontroversial, and suggest a declining demand for unskilled labour.[13]

Given the predictions of trade theory, it was natural to suspect that the growing trade with developing economies was one obvious explanation for the phenomenon of declining demand for unskilled labour.[14] A good deal of research effort, therefore, has been devoted to the exploration of the hypothesis and a large literature has emerged.[15] The basic conclusion that this literature suggests can be stated as follows. While imports of manufactured goods from low-income developing countries have been growing, they still constitute a very small proportion of total manufactured imports into industrialized countries. Thus, even though imports from low-income countries have had the effect of depressing the demand for unskilled labour, this effect has in reality been too

[13] See OECD (1994), for example, for a detailed review of the empirical evidence.

[14] Rodrik (1997) has argued that the growth of trade has also increased the insecurity of unskilled and low-skilled workers by making the demand for their services more sensitive to wages. As he recognizes, however, it is growth of trade in general, and not growth of trade with developing countries in particular, that is relevant in this context. We leave this issue out of account here since our focus is on North–South trade.

[15] Some of the more recent studies are: Wood (1994, 1995 and 1998); Dewatripont, Sapir and Sekkat (1999); Krugman (1995, 2000); Collins, ed. (1998); Cline (1997); and Slaughter (1998).

small to explain the growth of skill-related inequalities, which is an economy-wide phenomenon. Empirical evidence on the whole suggests that skill-biased technological change (and not trade with low-income countries) is the chief explanation for the job losses and the increase in the wage inequality.[16]

Our analysis, based on a recent ILO study, suggests a more qualified, though not fundamentally different, conclusion.[17] Tables 4.3 and 4.4 give a summary view of the trends in manufacturing employment and wages during 1980–96 in the seven countries covered by the study. The basic facts, highlighted by the tables, are as follows.

- Aggregate employment in manufacturing declined everywhere except in Germany (where employment growth was zero) and Japan (where employment continued to grow throughout the period). As a rule, wherever employment declined, it declined in both high-skill and low-skill industries though the decline was often sharper in low-skill industries.[18] Overall, it cannot be argued that job losses occurred only in low-skill industries.
- Real wage growth was substantial everywhere. Once again, wherever real wages grew, they grew in both high-skill and low-skill industries. The only exception was the United States, where the real wage growth was substantial in high-skill industries but zero in low-skill industries.[19]
- As a rule, the wage differential between high-skill and low-skill industries increased, though there were exceptions (the differential declined in Netherlands and the United Kingdom). This is implied by the data in table 4.4 and is explicitly shown in figure 4.1.

At first sight, it is hard to see how trade with developing countries could have had anything to do with these trends. Trade theory predicts a rising skill premium but does not predict declining employment in high-skill industries or rising real wages of low-skilled labour. Except in the United States, the rising skill premium does not seem to have been associated with stagnation of real wages of low-skilled labour and, as such, does not appear to be linked to trade with developing countries.

Indeed, the observed trends seem to be most consistent with the hypothesis of skill-biased technological change. If we accept this hypothesis, it would seem natural to suppose that skill intensity was rising in all industries and there

[16] See Acemoglu (2002) for a fairly comprehensive review of the arguments and the evidence.

[17] See Landesmann et al. (2002).

[18] There were important exceptions to the rule. In the Netherlands and the United States, employment decline was largely confined to high-skill industries, while in Germany it was largely confined to low-skill industries.

[19] This seems odd since in the United States employment declined in high-skill industries and not in low-skill industries. But, as we shall see later, wage changes had very little to do with changes in the demand for labour in any of the countries considered.

Table 4.3 Average annual growth (%) of employment, selected industrialized countries, various years

	Low-skill industries	Medium-skill industries	High-skill industries	All industries
France				
1980–95	–2.34	–1.78	–0.90	–1.86
1983–95	–2.27	–1.55	–1.03	–1.76
Germany				
1980–95	–1.45	0.12*	0.40*	–0.41
1983–95	–1.12	0.20	0.35*	–0.26*
Netherlands				
1980–95	–0.45	0.06*	–1.43	–0.42
1983–95	0.20*	0.43*	–1.32	0.01
Sweden				
1980–96	–2.43	–0.77	–1.97	–1.54
1983–96	–2.66	–1.22	–2.05	–1.84
United Kingdom				
1980–94	–2.10	–1.94	–1.37	–1.89
1983–94	–1.50	–0.94	–1.04	–1.18
United States				
1980–96	–0.40	–0.02*	–1.11	–0.41
1983–96	–0.08*	0.27	–1.59	–0.27
Japan				
1980–96	0.15*	1.02	1.18	0.67
1983–96	0.07	1.19	0.41*	0.54

Note: * statistically equivalent to zero. The classification scheme is explained in Appendix 4.1. Separate estimates for the period starting in 1983 are made in order to check for the effects of the second hike in petroleum prices in 1979.

Source: Estimated by the author on the basis of the database used in Landesmann et al. (2002).

was shedding of low-skilled labour in all industries in the process. The result would be growth of real wages in all industries, partly because of productivity growth (resulting from technology upgrading) and partly because of growth in the share of skilled workers in the total workforce. The rising ratio of the real wage in high-skill industries to that in low-skill industries could then result either from faster technological change in high-skill industries or from rising

Figure 4.1 Wage inequality in selected industrialized countries, 1980-96

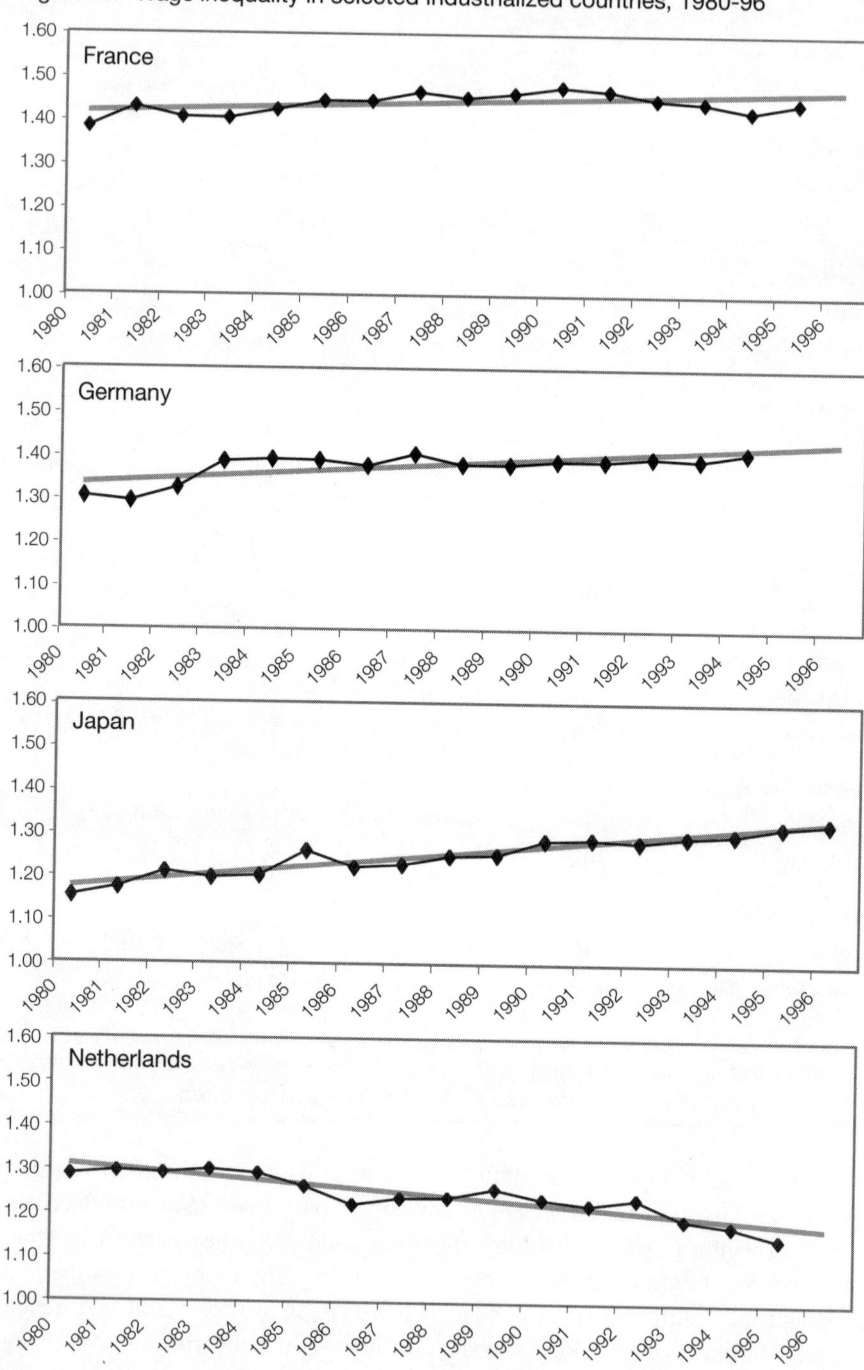

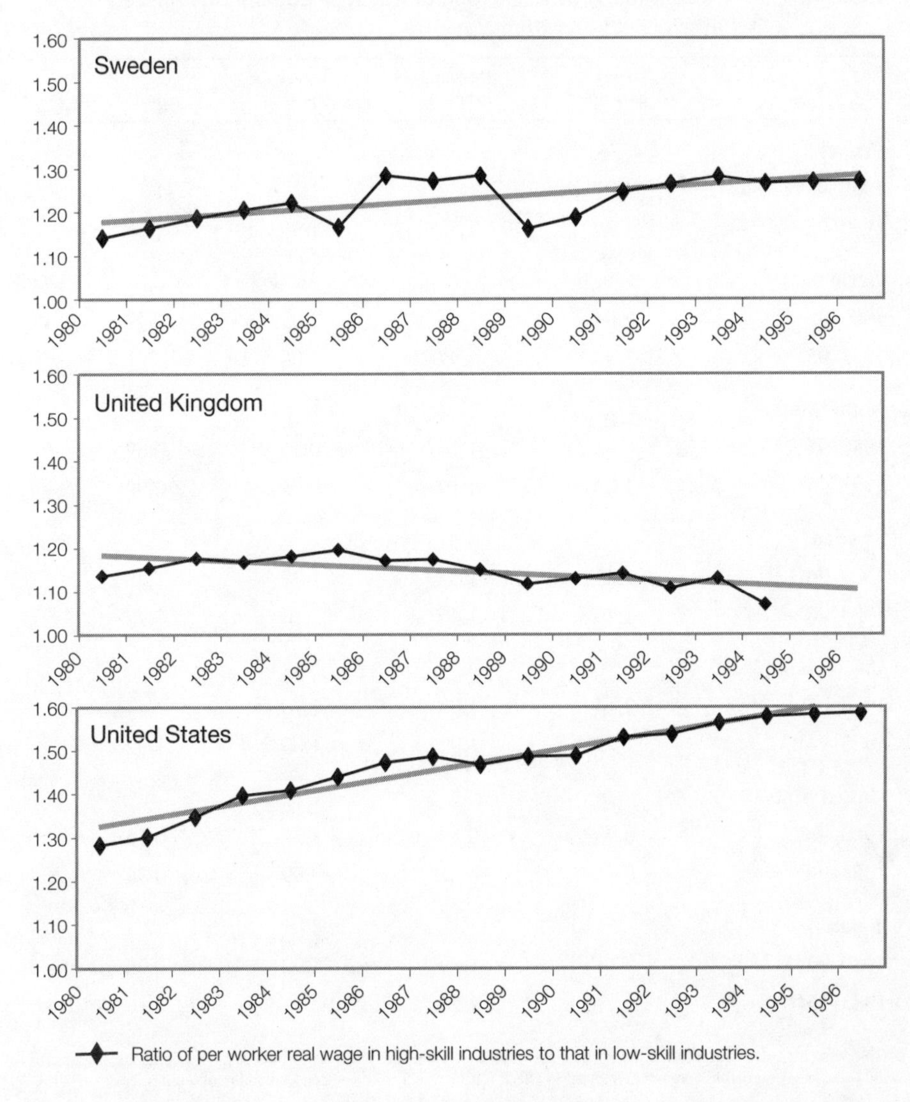

Source: Author's estimates based on the database in Landesmann et al. (2002).

skill premium in each category of industry, or from a combination of the two. If the skill premium were indeed rising, the explanation would lie in economy-wide labour market developments. Otherwise, it is hard to see why rising productivity should increase real wages of high-skilled and low-skilled labour at systematically different rates in the same industries.

Table 4.4 Average annual growth (%) of real wage, selected industrialized countries, various years

	Low-skill industries	Medium-skill industries	High-skill industries	All industries
France				
1980–95	1.27	1.32	1.49	1.41
1983–95	1.39	1.50	1.50	1.53
Germany				
1980–95	1.64	1.86	2.09	1.97
1983–95	1.99	1.97	2.08	2.11
Netherlands				
1980–95	0.96	1.16	0.26	0.89
1983–95	1.04	1.19	0.25	0.92
Sweden				
1980–96	1.43	1.25	1.98	1.48
1983–96	1.76	1.46	2.16	1.72
United Kingdom				
1980–94	2.14	1.65	1.70	1.84
1983–94	1.79	1.02	1.03	1.32
United States				
1980–96	0.05*	0.50	1.31	0.55
1983–96	0.01	0.32	0.99	0.36
Japan				
1980–96	2.13	1.89	2.92	2.26
1983–96	2.17	1.56	2.91	2.16

Note: * statistically equivalent to zero. The classification scheme is explained in Appendix 4.1. Separate estimates for the period starting in 1983 are made in order to check for the effects of the second hike in petroleum prices in 1979.

Source: Estimated by the author on the basis of the database used in Landesmann et al. (2002).

This interpretation of the trends has wide acceptance in the literature.[20] It also receives strong support from two main findings of the ILO study. The first finding is that while the growth of labour productivity was substantial in both low-skill and high-skill industries, it was faster in high-skill industries. Moreover, the growth

[20] See Acemoglu (2002). There are a few dissenting voices. Wood (1994, 1995), in particular, strongly argues that North–South trade has been a major cause of job losses and rising wage inequality in the North.

of labour productivity was in fact the principal explanation for the decline in employment and the sole explanation for the growth of real wages. The second finding is that the direct effect of trade with developing countries on employment and wages in manufacturing industries as a whole was close to zero.

The study shows that while the level of growth of import penetration from developing countries was highest in low-skill industries, the rate of growth of import penetration from those countries was highest in high-skill industries. However, an examination of the simultaneous changes in imports and exports in each group of industries shows that, vis-à-vis the developing countries, the industrialized countries became net importers of products of low-skill industries but remained net exporters of products of high-skill industries. These facts suggest that while the trade in low-skill products reflected a shift in comparative advantage, trade in high-skill products reflected a growth of outsourcing. The growth of outsourcing in high-skill industries is also suggested by the fact that the rapid growth of imports from developing countries was associated with equally rapid growth of exports to those countries.[21]

Detailed econometric analysis[22] shows that labour productivity growth was the most general cause of declining employment in all industries throughout the period. Thus the hypothesis that skill-biased technological change is the main explanation for the decline in manufacturing employment is quite strongly supported. However, in both low-skill and high-skill industries, as well as in manufacturing industries as a whole, import penetration from developing countries had a negative effect on employment in the 1980s (but not in the 1990s), independently of the effects of productivity growth. On the other hand, growth of manufactured exports to developing countries, which accompanied the growth of import penetration from those countries, had a positive effect on employment in manufacturing industries as a whole in both periods. It is thus clear that, in manufacturing industries as a whole, the direct (net) employment effect of trade with developing countries was ambiguous in the 1980s and positive in the 1990s, but basically small in both periods.

Interestingly, however, the positive employment effect of exports to developing countries is not observed specifically in high-skill or low-skill industries (which implies that the positive effect was confined to medium-skill industries). The most plausible reason is that these exports (in relation to output) were not significant in quantitative terms. Thus in both groups of industries, on balance, trade with developing countries had an adverse direct effect on employment of

[21] Other studies, which examine this aspect in much greater detail, support this view. See, for example, Arndt and Kierzkowski (2001). The case studies of selected developing countries, discussed below, also highlight the importance of outsourcing in high-skill industries.

[22] The results, not reported here, are available in Landesmann et al. (2002).

low-skilled labour in the 1980s. At the same time, the growth of exports to other industrialized countries had a positive direct effect on employment in high-skill industries. The obvious reason is that the industrialized world is where the major market for the final products of high-skill industries is located. Employment in high-skill industries in any particular country, therefore, depended on success in competition for market share in the industrialized world. It is thus arguable that it was trade among industrialized countries that was driving the growth in outsourcing from developing countries.

The key findings, therefore, are as follows. Trade with developing countries directly explains only a part of the decline in the employment in low-skill industries in the 1980s. At the same time, it also explains a part of the increase in the employment in medium-skill industries in both periods. The outsourcing-related decline in employment in high-skill industries is attributable as much to trade among industrialized countries as to trade with developing countries. In short, trade with developing countries had no significant effect on total manufacturing employment in industrialized countries[23] but changed its composition; the share of medium-skill industries increased while the shares of low-skill and high-skill industries declined. This change in composition also implies that the share of low-skilled employment in total manufacturing employment declined. So trade with developing countries hurt unskilled labour and benefited skilled labour, much as theory would predict.

But this is not the whole story. Since the general explanation for the observed decline in employment in manufacturing industries lies in productivity-enhancing technological innovations, we need to ask if trade with developing countries played a role in inducing the technological innovations. In principle, it could have played such a role in so far as it created a threat of competition from producers in developing countries, thereby inducing what is called defensive innovation in low-skill industries.[24] The seriousness of this effect is hard to guess because defensive innovation is not the only explanation for skill-biased technological change, which occurred in all types of industries. It has to be recognized, moreover, that trade with developing countries was not the only factor that could have induced defensive innovation in low-skill industries; there are good reasons to think that government policies have had the same effect. The

[23] One recent study of ten industrialized countries (Australia, Canada, Denmark, France, Germany, Italy, Japan, Netherlands, United Kingdom and United States) finds that trade with non-OECD countries (including Hungary, Poland, Mexico and Korea, Rep.) reduced manufacturing employment in each of the countries during 1978–95 (Kucera and Milberg, 2002). However, the methodology employed in this study, which is quite different from that employed in Landesmann et al. (2002), takes inadequate account of productivity growth.

[24] Defensive innovation refers to efforts by entrepreneurs either to upgrade products or to reduce costs through technological upgrading with a view to meeting anticipated competition from producers in developing countries. See Wood (1994) for a discussion.

low-skill industries in industrialized countries enjoyed, and still enjoy, a significantly higher-than-average degree of protection through higher-than-average tariffs as well as through quantitative restrictions and anti-dumping measures. And governments have often provided investment subsidies to these industries. It is arguable that this combination of protection and subsidies had the effect of promoting defensive innovation and hence hurt low-skill workers.[25]

Since skill-biased technological change was not confined to low-skill industries, there clearly were forces other than trade with developing countries that played a role in inducing it. The current consensus in the literature is that the rapid increase in the supply of skilled workers has itself induced the development of skill-complementary technologies.[26] But we also need to bear in mind that a productivity-driven process of deindustrialization had begun in most of the industrialized countries well before trade with developing countries started to grow (see Appendix 4.2),[27] that trade among industrialized countries (implying competition for market shares within the industrialized world) is likely to have been a factor inducing skill-biased technological change[28] and that the 1980s and the 1990s could plausibly be viewed as periods of exogenous technological advances.

Finally, the results of the econometric exercises reported in the ILO study show that neither the growth of import penetration from developing countries nor the growth of exports to those countries had any direct impact on wages. Wage growth was driven solely by labour productivity growth, which was substantial in all industries. The wage gap between high-skill and low-skill industries increased because of a widening of the productivity gap between them; productivity growth was faster in high-skill industries.[29] It cannot, of course, be known from this if the wage gap between high-skilled and low-skilled labour increased within each industry. Since wage growth was driven by productivity growth, there is in fact no reason to expect systematically different rates of wage growth for high-skilled and low-skilled labour in the same industry; it is not reasonable to suppose that

---

[25] Indeed, it can be argued that government policies intended to help low-skill industries were designed not to protect low-skilled jobs but to induce skill-biased innovations. See Milner (1988); OECD (1983); and Hufbauer, Berliner and Elliot (1986) for relevant facts and analysis.

[26] See Acemoglu (2002).

[27] Rowthorn and Ramaswamy (1997) provide an analysis of deindustrialization and reach the following conclusion (p. 22): "The most important factor that accounts for deindustrialization is the systematic tendency for productivity in manufacturing to grow faster than in services. North–South trade has played very little role in deindustrialization."

[28] Rowthorn and Ramaswamy (1997) find that trade among the industrialized countries accounts for the variation in the share of manufacturing in total employment from one industrialized country to another. Kucera and Milberg (2002) show that trade with other OECD countries reduced manufacturing employment in four countries (Australia, Japan, United Kingdom and United States) and increased it in the other six of the ten countries studied. What these findings indicate is that sustaining manufacturing employment requires surviving competition in OECD markets.

[29] The fact that wage inequality actually declined in the Netherlands and the United Kingdom implies that, in these countries, productivity growth was faster in low-skill than in high-skill industries.

the productivity of the two types of labour grew at systematically different rates. Thus whether the skill premium increased in manufacturing industries remains unclear.[30] But if it did increase, the explanation is most likely to be found in the economy-wide labour market developments.[31]

Employment and wages in developing countries

As already noted, surprisingly little research effort has so far been devoted to assessing empirically the impact of trade with industrialized countries on manufacturing employment and wages in developing countries.[32] Even the research that has been done suffers from some unhelpful biases. The selection of cases for study has been somewhat random, for example. Certain Central American countries have received much attention even though they are basically exporters of primary commodities, while certain Asian countries have received little attention even though they are major exporters of manufactures. Moreover, researchers have generally been more interested in studying the effect of trade on wage inequality than on studying the effect on employment and real wages. For all these reasons, we still do not have empirically well-founded propositions on the core issues of interest.

Trade theory, as outlined above, suggests that growth of manufactured trade with industrialized countries would increase employment – but not necessarily real wages – of unskilled labour in developing countries with dualistic labour markets. It is also quite clear, from our discussion in Chapter 2 of what we have called a process of global redistribution of manufacturing employment, that the general experience of the ME countries is consistent with at least a part of the prediction of theory; manufacturing employment in these countries as a group has shown rather impressive growth. However, the disaggregated picture is more complex. There are indications that the employment effect of trade has not in fact been favourable in all ME countries. Table 4.5 shows that in a sub-group of these countries and territories (Group 2) growth of trade was

[30] The evidence on trends in skill premium, available in the literature, usually refers to the economy-wide skill premium rather than to that in manufacturing industries.

[31] If the wage of low-skilled labour outside the manufacturing sector falls, then this might reduce the wage of low-skilled labour in manufacturing. Indeed, given that the bulk of the employment is in services, economy-wide changes in the skill premium are most likely to be explicable in terms of the developments in service industries. Changes in governments' labour market policies could also have been important factors. It has been argued that in the United States the rise in wage inequality, and particularly the stagnation of the real wage for unskilled labour, could have been partly due to the erosion of the government-determined real minimum wage (Lee, 1999). Immigration of low-skilled workers could also reduce the wage of low-skilled labour if immigrants do not receive the same labour market protection as local workers. Immigrants, for example, may increasingly fill the low-skill jobs while the local workers move up the scale. See Borjas and Freeman, eds. (1992).

[32] World Bank (2002) and Oxfam (2002) review most of the available studies. See also Wood (1994, 1997); Feenstra and Hanson (1997); Revenga (1995); Berman et al. (2000); and Ghose (2000).

Table 4.5 Manufacturing employment in ME countries and territories, 1980 and 1997

	Employment in millions		As % of total employment	
	1980	1997	1980	1997
Group 1	50.9	82.8	79.0	88.7
Group 2	13.5	10.6	21.0	11.3
Total	64.4	93.4	100.0	100.0

Note: Group 1 includes 15 ME countries and territories that showed rising manufacturing employment during the period: China, Egypt, India, Indonesia, Israel, Korea (Rep.), Malaysia, Mauritius, Morocco, Philippines, Singapore, Sri Lanka, Taiwan (China), Thailand and Turkey. Group 2 includes 7 ME countries and territories that showed stagnant or declining manufacturing employment during the period: Argentina, Brazil, Hong Kong (China), Malta, Mexico, Pakistan and South Africa. It should be noted that, in the case of Mexico, employment in maquiladora industries has been left out of account (maquiladora industries are discussed in detail on pp. 66–72); otherwise, it would have belonged to Group 1.

Source: Ghose and Matsumoto (2002).

associated with declining manufacturing employment. We should recall also that some of these countries achieved rather poor economic growth despite an impressive record in expanding manufactured exports, as discussed in Chapter 3. It turns out that the countries with poor growth performance were also those that failed to derive employment benefits from trade.[33]

These are, of course, broad observations that only set the stage for the analysis of employment and wage effects of manufactured trade that we present below. This analysis is based on the results available from a set of recent ILO studies.[34] The studies focus on five carefully selected developing countries, which emerged as major exporters of manufactures to industrialized countries over the last two decades: Brazil, China, India, Malaysia and Mexico. In all the countries, trade liberalization started in the mid-1980s and accelerated in the early 1990s. And though the nature and depth of liberalization varied,[35] both the trade–GDP ratio and the share of manufactures in total exports increased very substantially in each of the selected countries in the post-1985 period.[36]

Table 4.6 shows the main trends in manufacturing employment, wages and labour productivity (value added per worker) in the five countries since the mid-1980s. For reasons of data availability, the period covered could not be the same for all the countries studied. Also, the data do not cover the entire manufacturing

[33] Four of the countries in Group 2 – Argentina, Brazil, Mexico and South Africa – do not belong to the convergence club identified in Chapter 3.

[34] These are: Goldar (2002); Woo and Ren (2002); Rasiah (2002); Palma (2002); and Vernengo (2002).

[35] Detailed descriptions of the trade liberalization process in each of the countries are available in the studies cited in note 34 above.

[36] See Appendix 4.3.

Table 4.6 Average annual rate of growth (%) of employment, real wages and labour productivity in manufacturing in five ME countries, various years

	Employment	Real wage per worker	Labour productivity
Brazil, 1985–90			
Low-technology industries	0.03*	–0.75	–0.93
Medium–low-technology industries	0.04*	–0.66	–1.10
Medium–high-technology industries	0.03*	–0.69	–0.74
High-technology industries	0.13	–0.78	–0.55
Brazil, 1985–94			
Low-technology industries	–0.27	–0.59	–0.84
Medium–low-technology industries	–0.35	–0.49	–1.44
Medium–high-technology industries	–0.24	–0.45	–0.59
High-technology industries	–0.16	–0.49	–0.59
Brazil, 1990–94			
Low-technology industries	–0.40	0.57	0.07
Medium–low-technology industries	–0.68	0.81	0.68
Medium–high-technology industries	–0.21	0.77	0.84
High-technology industries	–0.34	1.01	0.94
China, 1984–95			
Export-oriented industries	3.44	5.04	2.95
Import-competing industries	2.22	5.87	4.31
Other industries	2.34	5.13	4.51
All industries	2.63	5.40	3.99
India, 1985–97			
Export-oriented industries	2.25	–0.19	5.03
Import-competing industries	2.72	1.79	7.64
Other industries (excluding petroleum)	2.92	1.39	6.07
Food, beverages and tobacco	3.19	1.88	4.52
All industries	2.76	1.17	6.42
India, 1990–97			
Export-oriented industries	3.36	–0.80	3.70
Import-competing industries	2.67	3.04	7.42
Other industries (excluding petroleum)	3.12	0.90	6.40
Food, beverages and tobacco	2.56	0.81	5.49
All industries	3.09	1.16	6.27

Malaysia, 1985–97			
Export-oriented industries	9.90	3.79	7.40
Other industries	8.10	3.52	6.60
Unskilled production workers	10.60	4.20	n.a.
Semi-skilled production workers	15.93	4.63	n.a.
Skilled production workers	9.58	4.16	n.a.
General workers	6.64	2.95	n.a.
Clerical and related workers	8.01	2.30	n.a.
Technical and supervisory staff	11.37	3.24	n.a.
Non-professional managerial staff	10.96	2.08	n.a.
Professional managerial staff	12.69	2.00	n.a.
Total, all industries	10.46	3.52	n.a.
Mexico, 1984–99			
Export-oriented industries	–1.79	2.08	4.49
Import-competing industries	–1.16	0.69*	3.76
Food, beverage and tobacco industries	0.15*	1.24	2.04
All non-maquiladora industries	–0.94	1.09	3.46
Maquiladora industries	11.02	–0.24*	–0.32*
All industries	1.31	0.36	1.80
Mexico, 1984–94			
Export-oriented industries	–0.61*	3.05	4.63
Import-competing industries	–0.28*	1.69	3.54
Food, beverage and tobacco industries	0.53	2.09	2.22
All non-maquiladora industries	–0.14*	2.10	3.48
Maquiladora industries	11.15	0.06*	–1.34
All industries	1.40	1.49	2.26

Note: * statistically equivalent to zero. The classification scheme used in the case of Brazil is the same as that in Appendix 4.1. The estimates for Brazil are based on simple averages of monthly statistics (index numbers).

n.a. = not available.

Source: Estimated by the author on the basis of the database used in Goldar (2002), Woo and Ren (2002), Rasiah (2002), Palma (2002), and Vernengo (2002).

sector; household and micro enterprises engaged in manufacturing are left out of account. For our purposes, this does not pose a major problem. The excluded enterprises account for only a small proportion of the manufacturing output in all the countries. And employment in such enterprises generally represents no more than survival strategies of the poor so that shrinkage rather than expansion of this type of employment is expected to be associated with development. Our data, on the other hand, cover much more than just enterprises in the regulated sector.

In the three Asian countries included in table 4.6, manufacturing output and employment grew at very impressive rates.[37] It is also clear that export expansion helped accelerate employment growth; employment growth was faster in export-oriented industries. We already know that export-oriented industries are significantly more unskilled-labour-intensive than import-competing industries in the cases of China and India, and this receives further confirmation from the fact that labour productivity and wages in import-competing industries are significantly higher than those in export-oriented industries.[38] So there is little doubt that employment of unskilled or low-skilled labour increased faster than that of skilled labour. In the case of Malaysia, the evidence is more direct. Employment of semi-skilled labour increased faster than that of other categories; this is consistent with the fact that outsourced products of high-technology industries are major items of Malaysia's exports.[39] Remarkably, employment in import-competing industries continued to grow at healthy rates in all three countries. This suggests that the growth of trade with industrialized countries has not had any significant adverse effect on the demand for skilled labour. In the case of Malaysia, the evidence directly shows that the growth of employment of skilled labour has not lagged far behind that of semi-skilled labour.

The detailed stories of China and India are in fact considerably more interesting than the simple facts indicate. In China in the early 1980s, nearly all urban workers (skilled and unskilled) were employed either in government agencies or in state-owned enterprises (SOEs), or in urban collectives (which effectively functioned as subsidiaries of SOEs); rural non-agricultural workers (mostly unskilled) were employed in township and village enterprises (TVEs); and rural–urban migration was very strictly controlled. The employees of SOEs (including government agencies) and of urban collectives enjoyed lifetime job tenure, while the employees of TVEs were contract workers. And the wage and income gaps between urban and rural workers were large. In the post-1985 period, the bulk of the new enterprises (mostly export-oriented) were TVEs. Moreover, even the SOEs and the urban collectives were allowed to employ new workers on a contract basis. Thus most of the new employees were contract workers, the bulk of them in TVEs. This also means that most of them were drawn from the pool of surplus unskilled workers in rural areas.

In India, the "other industries" are as unskilled-labour-intensive as the export-oriented industries and the food, beverage and tobacco industries are

[37] The rate of growth of output can be derived by adding the rate of growth of employment and the rate of growth of labour productivity.

[38] See figure 4.3.

[39] In 1997, electrical equipment and machinery accounted for 71 per cent of Malaysia's manufactured exports.

even more unskilled-labour-intensive than the export-oriented industries.[40] The import-competing industries, on the other hand, are the least unskilled-labour-intensive and most regulated.[41] That the employment of unskilled labour increased faster is evident from the fact that employment in both export-oriented and "other industries" grew faster than that in import-competing industries. All this also means that employment in regulated sector enterprises grew at a slower rate than that in enterprises outside the regulated sector. As in China, the bulk of the new employees in India were also drawn from the pool of surplus unskilled workers (though this surplus was not confined to rural areas since rural–urban migration has never been controlled in India).

In the two Latin American countries represented in table 4.6, the effects of trade seem to have been strikingly different. In Brazil, manufacturing employment stagnated during 1985–90, a period when some tentative steps towards trade liberalization were taken but trade openness actually declined; and it declined in the 1990s, a period of more substantive trade liberalization and growing openness.[42]

Even more strikingly, in the 1990s, employment not only declined in all branches of industry but also declined at a faster rate in low-skill industries. In other words, employment of both skilled and unskilled labour declined but that of unskilled labour declined at a faster rate.[43]

It thus appears that the effect of trade on manufacturing employment has been adverse in Brazil; also, it has been more adverse for unskilled labour than for skilled labour. A closer look does not alter this conclusion but shows a more complex picture. During 1985–90, manufacturing employment did not fall (in fact it rose in high-technology industries) even though output fell quite rapidly. So, while trade openness was declining, employment was sustained at the cost of falling labour productivity, and this was true for all categories of manufacturing industries. During 1990–94, when trade openness was growing, output continued to decline only in low-technology industries; output growth was slow but positive in the medium- and high-technology industries. Employment nevertheless shrank at a rapid rate in all industries while labour productivity grew. Thus there were three factors at work

[40] The ratio of labour productivity in food, beverage and tobacco industries to that in export-oriented industries was 0.69 for the period 1973–76, 0.56 for the period 1980–83 and 0.94 for the period 1996–98 (see Goldar, 2002).

[41] The petroleum-related industries are, of course, also skill-intensive and regulated, but they account for less than one per cent of total manufacturing employment (see Goldar, 2002).

[42] The period covered in the table is only 1985–94. This is clearly unsatisfactory, but it proved difficult to get access to more recent data at a disaggregated level. However, the observed trends for 1990–94, which are estimated from monthly data, are most likely to be valid for the whole of the 1990s. We know from the available statistics (not directly cited here) that the aggregate manufacturing employment declined at an annual rate of 0.52 per cent during 1990–99, a rate quite similar to that obtained for 1990–94.

[43] Given the level of disaggregation at which the data were available, it proved difficult to unambiguously distinguish export-oriented from import-competing industries; all industries seem to show substantial exports and imports. This is why a classification by technology has been preferred.

which reduced employment in general and that of unskilled labour in particular. The first was the stagnating manufacturing output, which we can plausibly suppose to have been linked to the general economic stagnation.[44] The second factor was the trade-induced restructuring, which seems to have changed the composition of manufacturing output in favour of medium- and high-technology industries. The third factor was labour hoarding in the pre-liberalization period; liberalization forced retrenchment of redundant labour.

Mexico's experience is unique in that its common border with the United States has allowed a rather spectacular growth of the so-called "maquiladora" industries: industries which process or assemble intermediate goods imported from the United States for exporting back to that country. However, the trade-induced changes in the non-maquiladora industries have not in fact been dissimilar to those observed in the case of the industries in Brazil in the 1990s. During 1984–99, employment in the non-maquiladora industries declined while output grew. Although the rate of this output growth was not particularly impressive, the growth of labour productivity in this period was remarkable. Moreover, within the non-maquiladora sector, relatively skill-intensive industries actually emerged as export-oriented industries.[45] And these export-oriented industries recorded the fastest decline in employment. Thus not only was the employment effect of trade in non-maquiladora manufacturing industries adverse, it was also more adverse in export-oriented industries than in import-competing or non-trading industries. It is not entirely clear if skilled and unskilled labour were affected differently. The trends in labour productivity indicate that the share of skilled labour in total employment was increasing, particularly in export-oriented and import-competing industries. On the other hand, employment did not decline in food, beverage and tobacco industries – the most unskilled-labour-intensive of all non-maquiladora industries. Perhaps it is safe to conclude that both skilled and unskilled workers were equally adversely affected.[46] As in Brazil, two factors seem to be have been at work in the context of non-maquiladora industries in Mexico as well: slow growth of output that reflected the slow growth of the economy,[47] and trade-induced restructuring that involved an increase in the share of skill-intensive industries in output.

The distinguishing feature of Mexico's experience is the phenomenal growth of maquiladora industries, in terms of both employment and output. It is this that

[44] Brazil's per capita GDP declined at a rate of 0.8 per cent per annum during 1985–94.

[45] The ratio of labour productivity in export-oriented industries to that in import-competing industries was 0.86 in 1980–82, 0.92 in 1990–92 and 0.95 in 1997–99. Cars overwhelmingly dominate the exports from the non-maquiladora sector. The food, beverage and tobacco industries are more unskilled-labour-intensive than both the export-oriented and the import-competing industries.

[46] The trends during the period 1984–94 were quite similar to those during 1984–99, except that employment did not decline during the former. It follows that employment in non-maquiladora industries declined rather sharply in the post-1994 period.

[47] Mexico's GDP per capita grew at a rate of only 0.7 per cent per annum between 1984 and 1999.

makes Mexico's industrial performance look respectable; in particular, the positive growth of manufacturing employment in the wake of trade liberalization was due solely to the growth of employment in maquiladora industries. Besides, these industries seem to have generated employment mainly for low-skilled labour; this is suggested by the fact that labour productivity in these industries has been and remains much lower than that in most non-maquiladora industries.[48] Thus when maquiladora and non-maquiladora industries are considered together, the observed employment effects of trade actually conform to expectations. The aggregate manufacturing employment grew and the employment of unskilled (or low-skilled) labour grew faster than that of skilled labour.[49]

The experiences of Brazil and Mexico raise two important questions for economists. First, why has growth performance of these countries been so poor in spite of their impressive trade performance? The answer probably lies in the problems carried over from the pre-liberalization period: the burden of external debt and the macroeconomic instability.[50] Second, why has trade promoted what appears to be the wrong kind of specialization? This question has received much attention in the literature, and several hypotheses have been proposed.[51] Satisfactory empirical substantiation of the hypotheses, however, requires much further research.

The trends in real wages in manufacturing, as shown by table 4.6, suggest the following conclusions.

- In general, the effect of trade on the real wage in manufacturing has been positive. In all five countries, real wages showed significant growth during periods of trade expansion.[52] Moreover, real wages grew for both unskilled and skilled labour.
- As a rule, the wage inequality within the manufacturing sector increased. These trends are clear from table 4.6, but are made clearer by figure 4.2. Malaysia was the exception to the rule.

---

[48] See figure 4.3.

[49] Mexico had an economic crisis in 1994, the same year that it joined the North American Free Trade Agreement (NAFTA). The crisis slowed down the growth of output in the non-maquiladora sector but not the growth of labour productivity. Thus employment in non-maquiladora industries declined quite sharply during 1994–99. At the same time, the growth of maquiladora industries remained unaffected. The economic crisis, together with NAFTA membership, thus sharpened the post-1984 trends. All this can be seen from a comparison of the trends during 1984–99 with those during 1984–94.

[50] In 1984, external debt constituted 54 per cent of GDP for Brazil and 59 per cent of GDP for Mexico; the debt service ratio (percentage of exports) was 45 per cent for each; and the rate of inflation was 192 per cent for Brazil and 65 per cent for Mexico. Gross domestic saving was significantly higher than gross domestic investment for the period 1984–93 in Brazil and for the period 1984–88 in Mexico, indicating substantial resource outflow. In both cases, the exchange rate was seen as an instrument for controlling inflation.

[51] Wood (1997) suggests that the rapid expansion of exports from large Asian countries such as China undermined the comparative advantage of the Latin American countries in unskilled-labour-intensive products. Revenga (1995) and Harrisson and Hanson (1999) suggest that, prior to liberalization, the unskilled-labour-intensive industries enjoyed a higher level of protection than the skill-intensive industries. The removal of protection, therefore, hurt the unskilled-labour-intensive industries much more. Feenstra and Hanson (1996, 2001) suggest that FDI, which was the driving force for the post-liberalization industrial restructuring, had the effect of promoting outsourcing in high-skill industries in the non-maquiladora sector.

[52] Brazil is the only case where real wages declined during 1985–94. But the decline occurred basically during 1985–90, a period when there was no trade expansion. Real wages grew in the 1990s, the period of growing openness and trade expansion.

Figure 4.2 Wage inequality in selected ME countries, various years.

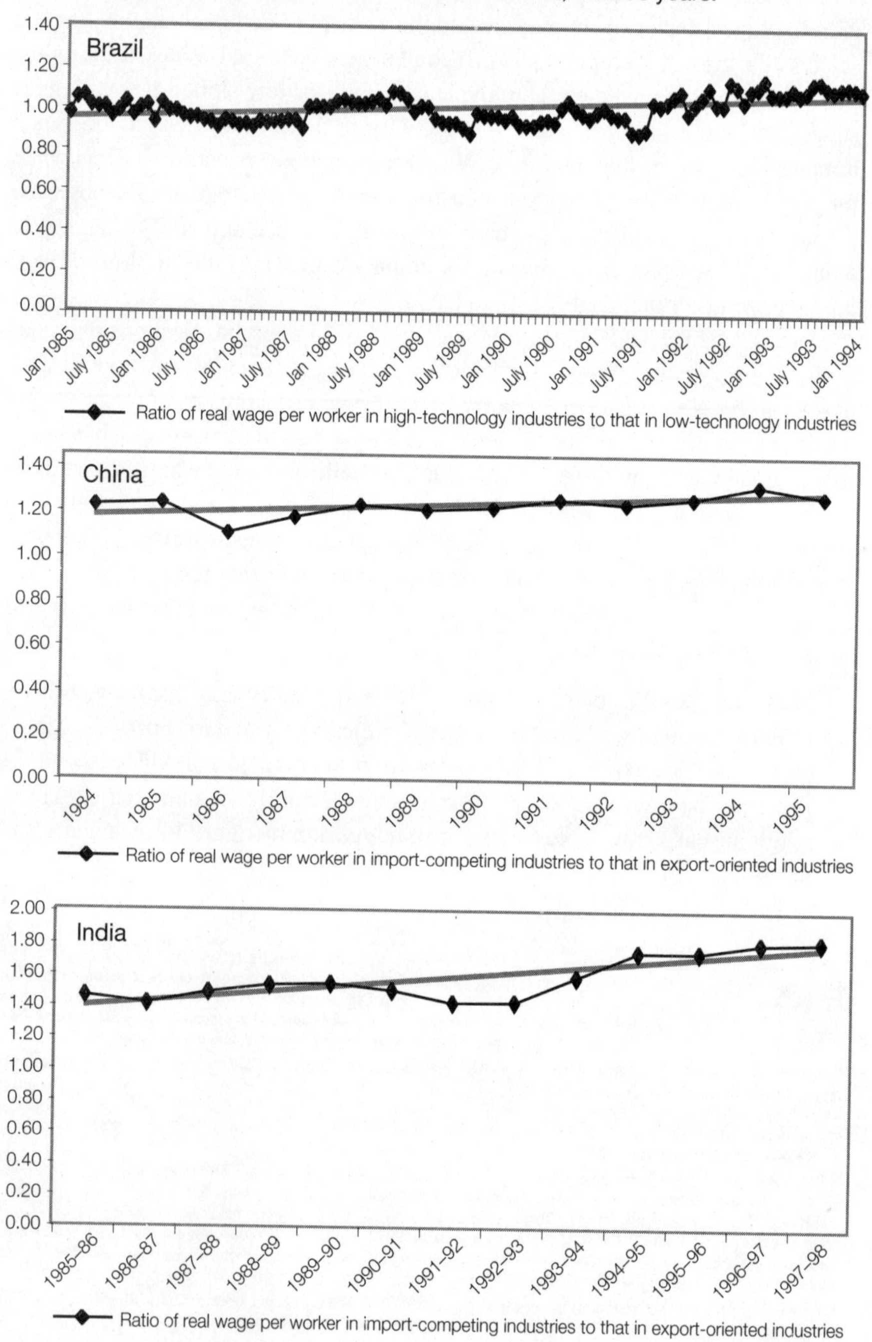

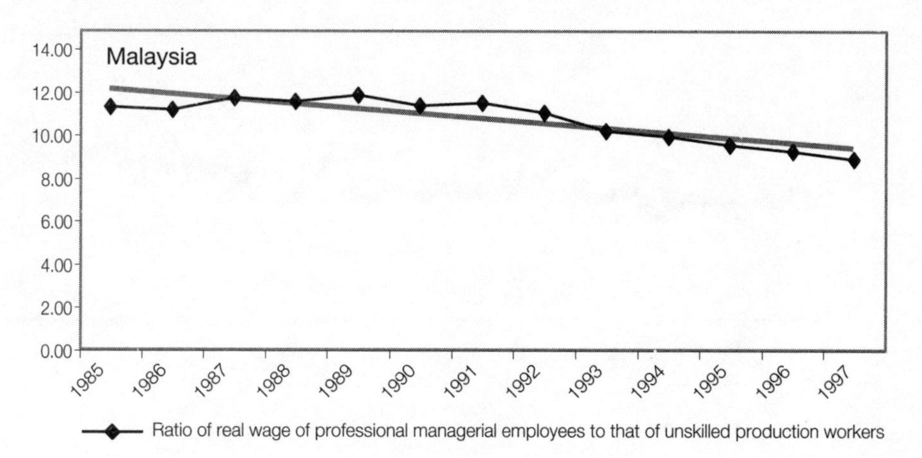

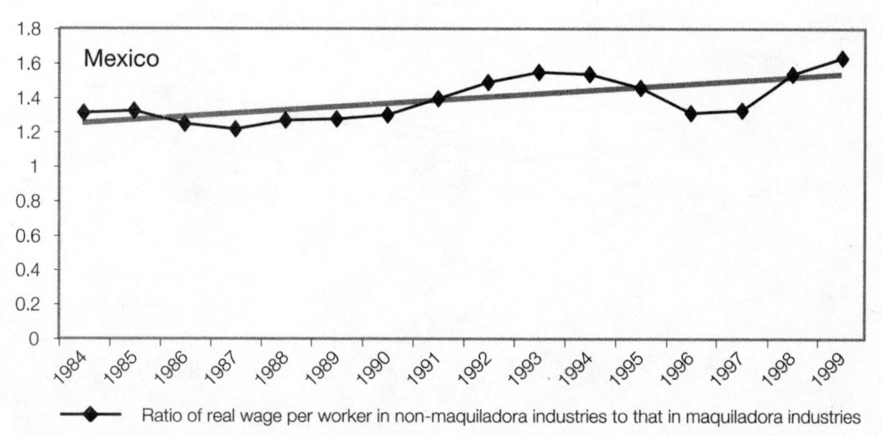

Note: For each country, the most appropriate indicator of wage inequality was chosen after a thorough examination of the data. In the case of Brazil, the data were index numbers of simple average real wage. In all other cases, they relate to weighted average real wage.

Source: Author's estimate based on the databases used in Goldar (2002), Woo and Ren (2002), Rasiah (2002), Palma (2002) and Vernengo (2002).

There are two cases that appear to suggest that the real wage of unskilled labour did not always increase. In India, the average real wage in export-oriented industries declined in spite of rapid growth of labour productivity. Did this mean a decline in the real wage of unskilled labour in manufacturing? The answer is no. As noted above, the food, beverage and tobacco industries are more unskilled-labour-intensive than the export-oriented industries. The fact that the average real wage in the food, beverage and tobacco industries showed

Figure 4.3 Inequality in labour productivity in selected ME countries, various years

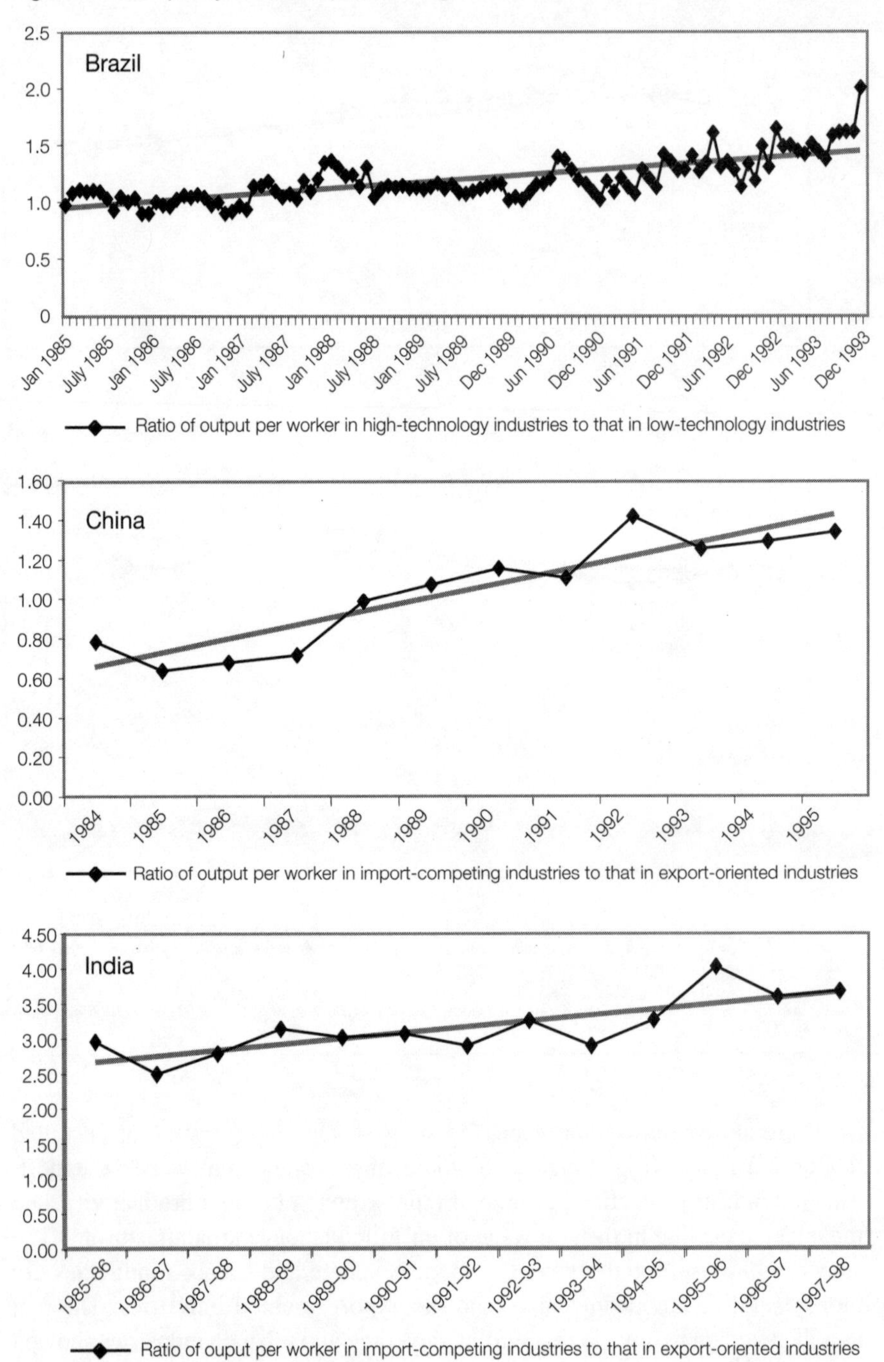

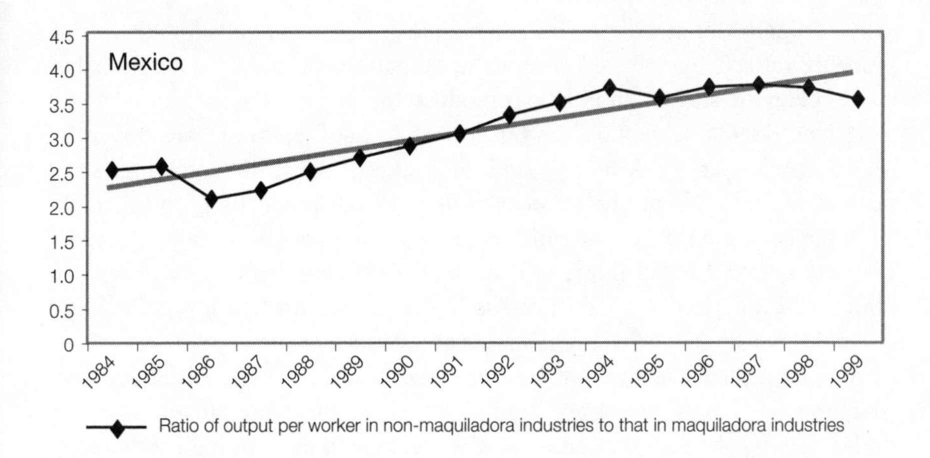

Note: For each country, the most appropriate indicator of wage inequality was chosen after a thorough examination of the data. In the case of Brazil, the data were index numbers of simple average labour productivity. In all other cases, they relate to weighted average real wage

Source: Author's estimate based on the databases used in Goldar (2002), Woo and Ren (2002), Rasiah (2002), Palma (2002) and Vernengo (2002).

significant growth suggests that the real wage of unskilled labour was actually rising. Why, then, did the average real wage in export-oriented industries decline? The reason is to be found in the process of restructuring in these industries that had been under way for some time and may have been speeded up by trade liberalization. In certain export-oriented industries, such as jute and cotton textiles, older large-scale enterprises were being replaced by newer medium- or small-scale enterprises;[53] this is reflected in the decline in the average employment per factory.[54] The result has been a decline in the proportion of regulated sector workers in total employment in export-oriented industries. It is this change in the composition of employment that has had the effect of reducing the average real wage, and this effect has clearly outweighed the effect of the rise in the real wage of unskilled labour in general.

In Mexico, the real wage in maquiladora industries remained unchanged throughout the period 1984–99. Once again, however, this need not necessarily mean that the real wage of unskilled labour stagnated. It turns out that the level of real wage in food, beverage and tobacco industries is very similar to that in maquiladora industries,[55] and this suggests that the former also employ mainly unskilled labour. Yet the real wage in food, beverage and tobacco industries

[53] See Howell and Kambhampati (1999).

[54] See Goldar (2002).

[55] The ratio of the average wage in food, beverage and tobacco industries to that in maquiladora industries was 0.94 in 1984–87, 0.97 in 1990–92 and 1.07 in 1997–99.

showed significant growth. So the stagnant real wage in maquiladora industries probably reflects unobserved changes in output composition, which probably also explain the stagnation in labour productivity.

A close look at table 4.6 shows that the growth of real wage was driven by growth of labour productivity. And this suggests that the growing wage inequality resulted from the faster growth of labour productivity in relatively skill-intensive industries. That this indeed was the case becomes very clear if we view figure 4.2 and figure 4.3 together. In Brazil, labour productivity in high-technology industries declined at a slower rate than in low-technology industries during 1985–90 and increased at a faster rate during 1990–94. These trends are reflected in the trends in real wages and in wage inequality; real wages declined in all industries during 1985–90 and increased in all industries during 1990–94, and the ratio of the average wage in high-technology industries to that in low-technology industries increased throughout the period 1985–94. In China and India, the ratio of the average wage in (skill-intensive) import-competing industries to that in (unskilled-labour-intensive) export-oriented industries increased because labour productivity increased faster in the former.[56] In Mexico, the rising wage inequality meant a rising ratio of the average wage in non-maquiladora industries to that in maquiladora industries. Underlying this trend is the fact that labour productivity was growing quite rapidly in the former but tended to decline in the latter.[57]

We conclude that the generally faster productivity growth in relatively skill-intensive industries explains why the wage inequality in manufacturing was rising. There are two related points that are worth emphasizing. First, changes in demand for labour seem to have had little to do with the growth of wage inequality; this is clear from the fact that the employment trends associated with the growth of wage inequality were quite different in different countries.[58] Second, the growth of wage inequality occurred in a context where real wages were generally rising. There is no case where the real wage was falling for any particular category of workers while rising for others. And the only case where real wages fell was in Brazil during 1984–90, but they fell in all types of industries and (by implication) for all categories of workers.

---

[56] The exceptional case of declining wage inequality in Malaysia seems to have been produced by certain unusual circumstances. The high weight of outsourced high-technology products in its exports explains the faster pace of productivity growth in the export-oriented industries, a majority of whose workers are semi-skilled. Moreover, Malaysia actually had a scarcity rather than a surplus of unskilled labour (in the 1990s, it became an important destination for unskilled migrant workers from its neighbours) and this helped reduce the wage inequality.

[57] The declining labour productivity in maquiladora industries is an intriguing fact that remains unexplained in the literature.

[58] In China and India, the context was one of rapid expansion of manufacturing output and employment, while it was one of stagnation in Brazil and Mexico. Thus changes in labour demand clearly did not have much to do with the wage trends. The same pattern, it may be recalled, was observed in the case of industrialized countries as well.

A summing up

The direct effect of trade in manufactures with developing countries on aggregate manufacturing employment in industrialized countries has been close to zero. But the effect has been negative for low-skilled labour and positive for high-skilled labour, much as the mainstream trade theory would predict. The industrialized countries lost their comparative advantage in certain unskilled-labour-intensive industries. And, in high-skill industries, there was growth of outsourcing of unskilled-labour-intensive intermediate products from developing countries by firms in industrialized countries. On the other hand, the manufactures-exporting developing countries also served as expanding markets for exports of skill-intensive products from industrialized countries.

It is not the case, however, that only the trade with developing countries has had adverse effect on employment of low-skilled labour in industrialized countries. The growth of outsourcing was largely a consequence of competition in the context of trade among industrialized countries. In several cases, governments' attempts to protect the low-skill industries also had a negative impact on low-skill employment because they induced defensive innovation. And the pervasive skill-biased technological change, which strengthened the long-term trend towards deindustrialization, was in fact the most important development that reduced low-skill employment.

For manufactures-exporting developing countries, the employment effect of trade with industrialized countries has not been uniform. In particular, there are rather striking differences between the Asian and the Latin American countries. In Asian countries such as China, India and Malaysia, trade helped accelerate the growth of manufacturing employment; trade expansion was associated with accelerated growth of manufacturing output and rising share of unskilled labour in manufacturing employment. Remarkably, moreover, trade expansion has not hurt skilled labour, as it has not adversely affected the growth of output in import-competing industries, possibly because the high rate of economic growth created space for both increased imports and increased domestic production.

In Latin American countries such as Brazil and Mexico, the effect of trade on manufacturing employment has been much less favourable; aggregate manufacturing employment declined in Brazil and increased only slowly in Mexico. An important reason is that trade expansion occurred in a context of general economic stagnation in both countries, which ensured stagnation or slow growth of manufacturing output. The problems of macroeconomic management that they carried over from the pre-liberalization period made their economic growth and stability much too contingent on steady inflows of substantial FDI.

This made it difficult to sustain consistently high rates of economic growth. A second reason is that trade failed to promote specialization in unskilled-labour-intensive products; this is a feature that remains to be adequately explained, but may not be unrelated to the dependence on inflows of FDI. In both Brazil and the non-maquiladora sector of Mexico, liberalization of trade and investment led to a relative decline of low-technology industries and to the emergence of medium-high-technology industries as export-oriented industries. Trade, therefore, hurt low-skilled labour. The trends were modified in the case of Mexico by the very rapid growth of maquiladora industries, which generated employment mainly for low-skilled labour. Nevertheless, even in Mexico, the growth of aggregate manufacturing employment and of low-skilled employment remained far less impressive than in the three Asian countries.

Globally, two particular trends stand out. First, the trade-induced redistribution of manufacturing employment from industrialized to a group of developing countries has had the net effect of increasing global manufacturing employment; the employment gain in developing countries has been much larger than the employment loss in industrialized countries. Second, the employment effect of trade in most of the manufactures-exporting developing countries was positive and substantial.

One important finding is that trade had no direct effect on real wages in either industrialized or developing countries. In both groups of countries, real wage growth was driven by the growth of labour productivity. Also, in both groups of countries, the growth of labour productivity was significant in both low-technology and high-technology industries, but it was faster in the latter. Indeed, the fact that these trends are observed in both industrialized and developing countries suggests that skill-biased technological change was universally important, perhaps because trade served as a mechanism for international diffusion of technology. These developments explain the two quite general tendencies relating to real wage movements. First, real wages grew in both industrialized and developing countries, and usually for both low-skilled and high-skilled labour. Second, the wage inequality increased in both industrialized and developing countries. However, wage inequality in this context means inter-industry wage inequality. It remains unclear if the wage inequality between skilled and unskilled labour in manufacturing industries also increased.

What our findings underline is the fact that trade in today's world is much more than exchange of final products. Development of global production systems and global diffusion of technology are important correlates of trade. The observed employment and wage effects of trade in manufactures between industrialized and developing countries reflect the combined effects of shifting comparative advantage, growth of outsourcing and diffusion of skill-biased technological change.

It is clear that the popular concern in industrialized countries about the labour market effects of trade with developing countries is not well founded in empirical reality. Though the growth of this trade undoubtedly had a negative effect on employment of low-skilled labour, the effect has been small. A larger negative effect derived from skill-biased technological change. Government policies toward the low-skill industries also seem to have hurt low-skill employment. The growth of wage inequality, too, cannot be viewed as a consequence of trade with developing countries. Its explanation lies in the pattern of technological change across industries. This also means that, in the context of manufacturing industries, it is basically the inter-industry wage inequality that has increased. The growth of wage inequality between high-skilled and low-skilled labour seems to have occurred primarily outside the manufacturing sector. As such, it is attributable to economy-wide labour market developments engendered by the governments' labour market and immigration policies.

The popular concern about trade with industrialized countries generating poor-quality jobs and poverty in manufactures-exporting developing countries is also not well founded. It is true that, in most countries, much of the incremental employment of low-skilled labour in export-oriented industries has been outside what we have called the regulated sector, and hence is not of desirable quality. But it is equally true that the quality of this employment is significantly better than the previous employment of the workers involved.[59] Also, employment in export-oriented industries is often of better quality than other types of regular or irregular employment outside the regulated sector. In India, for example, employment in export-oriented industries is of better quality than that in food, beverage and tobacco industries. And it is of much better quality than the irregular or casual wage-employment that a large section of the workers must depend on. In Mexico too, employment in maquiladora industries is of no worse quality than that in food, beverage and tobacco industries. The fact that jobs in export-oriented industries are not always of desirable quality (by some absolute standard) should not obscure the fact that they often are of better quality than the jobs they replace and than other jobs elsewhere in the economy. Job creation of this type reduces poverty. It is the destruction of jobs or the absence of job growth that increases poverty. It is not accidental that poverty has

[59] This, of course, is obvious since if it were not the case the workers would not have taken up this employment. Still, there is also empirical evidence that substantiates the point: see Oxfam (2002), Moran (2002), and ILO (1998), for example.

been steadily declining in China, India, Malaysia and Mexico but has shown a tendency to rise in Brazil.[60] Brazil is the only country in our sample in which increased trade has been associated with reduced employment, particularly of low-skilled labour, in manufacturing industries.

While the popular concerns seem to be largely unfounded, our analysis indicates other areas of concern that merit attention. The first is that the effect of trade on manufacturing employment has not been favourable in some manufactures-exporting developing countries, particularly in those of Latin America. Our analysis of the experiences of Brazil and Mexico suggests that one reason for this is that their integration into the global economy occurred in a context of general economic stagnation, engendered by long-sustained macroeconomic imbalances. Another reason is that trade seems to have promoted the wrong kind of specialization in these countries, specialization that is not consistent with their comparative advantage. These are important issues that deserve serious investigation.

A second area of concern arises from the fact that trade does increase what is sometimes called labour market "churning" (simultaneous creation and destruction of jobs) in both industrialized and developing countries. The churning effect is naturally larger and more disruptive in countries where the employment effect of trade is negative or small, but it is present even in countries where the employment effect is positive and substantial. Moreover, in most countries, churning seems to hurt primarily the low-skilled labour. Appropriate labour market policies are required to counter the disruptive effects of churning, and it is not clear that such policies are in place in the countries concerned. Indeed, the labour market policies in industrialized countries seem to have accentuated rather than countered the disruptive effects of churning.

Finally, it is a disconcerting fact that both popular concerns and economists' debates have so far focused almost exclusively on the integrating economies, industrialized and developing. Yet there is little doubt that it is in the globally excluded countries that trade has had truly adverse effects on jobs and incomes in recent periods. And in these cases the explanation for the adverse effects lies, rather obviously, in the declining international prices of primary commodities, which, ironically, is also thought to have contributed positively to the growth of the global economy. A vicious circle can be glimpsed and the issue deserves far more attention than it has received so far. It is vitally important to recognize that the source of the most worrying problems of the global economy is not the new kind of North–South trade in manufactures but the traditional North–South trade in non-competing products.

---

[60] See Chen and Wang (2001); Datt and Ravallion (2002); Ferreira and Paes de Barros (1999); and Sala-i-Martin (2002).

APPENDIX 4.1

Classification of manufacturing industries

SIC rev.2 Code	Industry	Technology		Skill intensity	
		Rank	Category	Rank	Category
3845	Aircraft	1	HT	3	HS
3825	Office and computing equipment	2	HT	1	HS
3522	Drugs and medicines	3	HT	2	HS
3832	Radio, TV and communication equipment	4	HT	7	HS
3850	Professional goods	5	MHT	6	HS
3843	Motor vehicles	6	MHT	12	MS
383X	Electrical machines, excluding communication equipment	7	MHT	5	HS
3512X	Chemicals, excluding drugs	8	MHT	8	MS
3842A	Other transport	9	MHT	16	LS
382X	Non-electrical machinery	10	MHT	10	MS
3556A	Rubber and plastic products	11	MLT	18	LS
3841	Shipbuilding and repairing	12	MLT	4	HS
3900	Other manufacturing	13	MLT	15	LS
3720	Non-ferrous metals	14	MLT	13	MS
3600	Non-metallic mineral products	15	MLT	19	LS
3810	Metal products	16	MLT	14	MS
3534A	Petroleum refineries and products	17	MLT	9	MS
3710	Ferrous meals	18	MLT	17	LS
3400	Paper, products and printing	19	LT	11	MS
3200	Textiles, apparel and leather	20	LT	22	LS
3100	Food, beverages and tobacco	21	LT	20	LS
3300	Wood products and furniture	22	LT	21	LS

Note: The criterion for ranking by technology is "expenditure on research and development and on technology acquisition as % of output value". The criterion for ranking by skill intensity is "white-collar skilled workers as % of all workers". The technology categories are: high technology (HT), medium-high technology (MHT), medium-low technology (MLT) and low technology (LT). The skill intensity categories are: high skill (HS), medium skill (MS) and low skill (LS)

Source: For rankings and categories by technology, see OECD, *Main industrial indicators 1980–97*, www1.oecd.org/dsti/sti/stat-ana/stats/mi2_99_cde.pdf. For rankings and categories by skill intensity, see Landesmann et al. (2002).

Appendix 4.2

Ratio of manufacturing employment to total civilian employment, average annual growth rate (%), various years

	1970–79	1980–89	1990–99
France	–0.71	–2.26	–1.84
Germany	–1.15	–0.73	–3.45
Netherlands	–2.39	–1.35	–2.93
Sweden	–1.22	–0.98	–0.58*
United Kingdom	–1.84	–1.78	–2.25
United States	–1.58	–1.78	–2.25
Japan	–1.37	–0.25	–1.83

Note: * statistically equivalent to zero.

Source: Estimated by the author by using the data available from OECD.

Appendix 4.3

Trade performance of five ME countries, various years

	1984–86	1989–91	1996–98
Brazil			
Merchandise trade–GDP ratio (%)	17.9	13.0	14.8
Manufactured exports as % of total merchandise exports	44.6	53.8	53.3
China			
Merchandise trade–GDP ratio (%)	20.9	34.3	40.7
Manufactured exports as % of total merchandise exports	48.8	70.5	85.7
India			
Merchandise trade–GDP ratio (%)	11.3	12.1	16.9
Manufactured exports as % of total merchandise exports	57.8	68.3	74.4
Malaysia			
Merchandise trade–GDP ratio (%)	93.3	139.1	171.1
Manufactured exports as % of total merchandise exports	30.1	54.5	77.0
Mexico			
Merchandise trade–GDP ratio (%)	23.1	25.8	60.1
Manufactured exports as % of total merchandise exports	26.7	46.8	81.3

Source: Ghose and Matsumoto (2002).

TRADE AND INTERNATIONAL MIGRATION 5

Introduction

There is much public concern and debate about international migration, but it is not related to the concerns about globalization, at least not as yet. International migration worries many people in industrialized countries because they feel that immigrants pose a threat to their way of life. It is widely believed that immigrants not only undermine employment prospects and wages of nationals but also threaten social cohesion and cultural identity. In much of the developed world, social and political resistance to immigration is strong and this forces governments to adopt and maintain severely restrictive immigration policies.

To economists, such policies appear as strangely anomalous in an era when much effort is being made to promote freer cross-border flows of commodities and capital. Economic analysis has not found strong empirical support for the idea that immigration undermines job prospects and wages of nationals in industrialized countries.[1] Research has unearthed the fact that international migration was a central feature of the nineteenth century globalization.[2] And the current pattern of demographic change across countries (as shown in Chapter 3) is generating massive labour surpluses in the developing world and labour scarcity in the developed world simultaneously.[3] On the whole, therefore, the restrictive immigration policies of the developed world seem to reflect unfounded fears and apprehensions but impose real constraints on the development of the global economy.[4]

Given this context, in this chapter we focus on economists' central concern, namely the linkage between international trade and international migration.[5]

[1] See Borjas (1994, 1995); and Zimmermann (1995).

[2] See O'Rourke and Williamson (1999).

[3] See United Nations (2000) for a detailed picture.

[4] See, for example, the papers in Faini, de Mello and Zimmermann, eds. (1999); Nayyar (2000); and World Bank (2001).

[5] The analysis that follows draws on a recent ILO study by Ghose (2002).

Are there *a priori* reasons to think that growth of international trade calls for growth of international migration? And what does the available empirical evidence suggest?

Trade and international migration: Insights from economic theory

Economic analysis of international migration starts from the premise that workers move across national frontiers in search of higher incomes (wages) and better working conditions.[6] This is why labour flow is expected to be from the less developed to the more developed countries, from developing South to industrialized North in schematic terms. The existing North–South gap in labour incomes (wages, working conditions and social security arrangements) and the availability of information on this gap are among the major determinants of the potential level of international migration. Migratory pressures increase when either the gap in labour incomes rises, or more information on the gap becomes available, or both happen. But migration also involves substantial transportation, communication and search costs for the individuals concerned. Hence migratory pressures also depend on changes in these costs; they rise when costs decline (as a result of advances in technology, for example).[7]

Given the premise, the standard trade theory predicts that growth of international trade would reduce international migration and, conversely, increased international migration would reduce trade.[8] According to this theory, trade occurs because countries differ in terms of endowments of capital and labour – the basic factors of production. Differences in factor endowments cause differences in factor incomes under autarky; capital incomes are lower and labour incomes higher in the capital-abundant North than in the labour-abundant South.[9] On the one hand, this means that there are incentives for both capital and labour to move, though in opposite directions, in search of higher incomes. On the other hand, the price differences are also the source of comparative advantage. The labour-abundant South enjoys a comparative advantage in the

[6] In the real world, much of the international migration occurs for non-economic reasons such as natural disasters, social conflicts and political instability. This type of migration, however, is random in character and does not lend itself to systematic analysis.

[7] There are, moreover, substantial "disutility" costs associated with relocation of individuals from their own social–cultural–linguistic context to an alien one. In conceptual terms, these costs set natural limits to international migration. A world where migratory pressures have ceased to exist will still be an unequal world.

[8] The reference here is to the Heckscher–Ohlin version of the theory of comparative advantage. See Ghose (2002) for more details and references.

[9] A simplifying assumption is being used here. There is no need to think in terms of differences in absolute levels of incomes. All that is required is that the income of capital relative to that of labour is lower in the capital-abundant country and the opposite is true in the labour-abundant country.

production of those goods whose production uses labour more intensively. The capital-abundant North has a comparative advantage in the production of those other goods whose production uses capital more intensively. Trade occurs because both countries can benefit from it.

Obviously, if capital and labour were to move freely across borders, the differences in factor endowments would tend to disappear. So the basis for mutually beneficial trade would disappear as well. Free movement of factors, therefore, undermines trade. But consider what happens if capital and labour cannot move freely across borders and mutually beneficial trade occurs. As trade grows, the demand for capital (and hence capital incomes) would rise in the capital-abundant North and the demand for labour (and hence labour incomes) would rise in the labour-abundant South. So North–South differences in factor incomes would narrow. Growth of international trade, therefore, would weaken the incentives for both capital and labour to move; trade undermines migration.[10]

The problem with these arguments is that they are not consistent with real-world experiences. During the nineteenth century globalization, growth of trade was associated with growth of both capital flow and international migration. The current process of globalization, too, is characterized by simultaneous growth of trade and capital flow. So at least trade and capital flow do not seem to be substitutes. There is a mismatch between theory and reality.

This mismatch does not arise if a more modern variant of the theory of comparative advantage (outlined in Chapter 4) is used. In this variant, capital is assumed to be mobile across countries so that differences between countries are not in terms of endowments of capital and labour but in terms of endowments of skilled and unskilled labour. North is abundant in skilled labour and South is abundant in unskilled labour. To be realistic, we can assume that in skill-abundant North wages of both skilled and unskilled labour are higher than in the South, but that the wage of skilled labour relative to that of unskilled labour is lower.[11] In the initial situation, there are incentives for both skilled and unskilled labour to migrate from South to North. But mutually beneficial trade is also possible if the North specializes in skill-intensive products (that it can produce more cheaply than the South) and the South specializes in labour-intensive products (that it can produce more cheaply than the North).

Once again, if labour (skilled and unskilled) were to move freely across borders, the basis for mutually beneficial trade would tend to disappear because

[10] These are the arguments that persuaded the ILO to recommend to its member States the promotion of trade as a means to reduce migratory pressures. See Ghose (2002), p. 25, footnote 50.

[11] This means that the North–South gap in labour incomes is smaller for skilled labour than for unskilled labour.

movements would continue till both absolute and relative wages were equal in both countries. But, in the absence of free cross-border movement of labour, growth of trade would have rather peculiar effects on the incentives for migration. As trade grew, the demand for skilled labour would rise in the skill-abundant North and the demand for unskilled labour would rise in the unskilled-labour-abundant South. The North–South gap in labour incomes would therefore decline for unskilled labour and increase for skilled labour. Thus trade would weaken the incentive for unskilled labour to migrate but would strengthen it for skilled labour. There is something more to be said. If migration of skilled labour were permitted, the North would become even more skill-abundant and the South would become even more labour-abundant; the initial comparative advantage would be strengthened for each. So there would be more trade and hence new incentive for skilled labour to migrate. Trade and migration of skilled labour would be mutually reinforcing.

In this framework, then, the growth of North–South trade creates pressures for increased migration of skilled labour and for reduced migration of unskilled labour. It cannot be said *a priori* whether pressures for migration in general would increase or decline as a consequence.

These predictions of the mainstream trade theory are reassuring and worrying at the same time. Globalization, it seems, need not increase migratory pressures, and this is reassuring for those in industrialized countries who worry about the social consequences of immigration. But globalization could also generate an important problem of human capital flight, or brain drain, from developing countries. This is deeply worrying because the short- and long-run costs of brain drain are likely to be substantial for developing countries. Higher education is heavily subsidized in these countries and skilled migrants carry away scarce human capital built through public investment.[12] The growth of trade, if it creates a serious, self-sustained problem of brain drain, would make accumulation of human capital extremely difficult for many developing countries. And, as modern growth theory emphasizes, failure to accumulate human capital would gravely harm their long-run growth prospects.

But are the predictions of theory consistent with empirical evidence?

---

[12] Remittances are widely seen as the principal benefit of migration to source countries. But skilled migrants are in fact less likely to send remittances than unskilled migrants. The reason is that skilled migrants are from relatively well-off households that do not require income support on a regular basis. There are, of course, examples of contribution by skilled migrants to the development of their home countries through investment and knowledge sharing. There are also examples of return migration of skilled workers. However, all this typically happens after the migrants' home countries have already acquired economic dynamism.

International migration in the 1990s: The evidence

There clearly are two questions that we need to answer empirically.[13] First, what has been the trend in migration from developing to industrialized countries in the 1990s? The answer to this question should tell us if there are any signs of increased migratory pressures in the period of globalization. Second, is brain drain a significant problem and also on the rise? The answer to this question should tell us if we would need to worry about the consequences of freer movement of labour across national boundaries.

The trends

The basic data on the stock of legal immigrant workers from developing countries in the industrialized world are put together in table 5.1. There are four observations that can be made on the basis of these data. First, the quantitative significance of migration from developing countries is small. In 1998, the latest year for which we have estimates, the stock of migrant workers from the developing world was just over 17 million, representing 4.4 per cent of the workforce of the industrialized world. This also means that a negligible proportion, just around 0.8 per cent, of the workforce of the developing world had migrated to work in industrialized countries. Second, in the 1990s, the main destination for migrant workers from developing countries was the United States, which by 1998 accounted for 75 per cent of all immigrant workers from developing countries working in the industrialized world. Only 13 per cent of these workers were in Western Europe. Third, the rate of growth of the immigrant workforce (from developing countries) during the decade 1988–98 was 7.5 per cent per annum, much higher than the rate of growth (0.8 per cent per annum) of the non-immigrant workforce of the industrialized world. Consequently, immigrants as a percentage of the workforce increased from 2.3 to 4.4. Once again, the United States, where immigrants as a percentage of the workforce increased from 4.9 in 1988 to 9.7 in 1998, stands out as the most important host country. In Western Europe, the rate of growth of the immigrant workforce was low (2.5 per cent per annum), and immigrants as a percentage of the workforce barely increased (it was 1.1 in 1988 and 1.3 in 1998). Finally, average annual legal immigration from developing countries, during the decade, was 0.9 million, 0.7 million into the United States alone.

[13] It has to be said that the available statistical data on international data are rather sketchy. They also suffer from limitations as the definitions adopted and the methods used for collection and compilation of statistics are not uniform across countries. We have tried to minimize these limitations through a process of careful selection. See Ghose (2002) for the details.

Table 5.1 Stock of migrant workers from developing countries, 1988 and 1998

	Stock (in thousands)		As % of workforce	
	1988	1998	1988	1998
Western Europe	1 764	2 264	1.1	1.3
United States	5 777	13 041	4.9	9.7
Australia	397	579	4.9	6.0
Canada	179	1 019	1.3	6.2
Japan	246	389	0.4	0.6
Total	**8 363**	**17 292**	**2.3**	**4.4**

Note: Western Europe includes Austria, Belgium, Denmark, Finland, France, Germany, Italy, Netherlands, Norway, Portugal, Spain, Sweden, Switzerland and the United Kingdom.

Source: Ghose (2002).

Two broad conclusions emerge from the facts. First, the share of immigrants in the total workforce rose in industrialized countries not because there was a flood of immigrant workers but because the non-immigrant workforce grew very slowly, reflecting the demographic changes under way. Second, emigration for work had negligible effect on the growth of the workforce in developing countries.

There is, moreover, evidence to show that the annual level of legal immigration from developing into industrialized countries was declining during the 1990s. Table 5.2 presents the available data on annual inflows of the migrant population from developing countries into a group of industrialized countries. Clearly, the annual inflow increased between 1988 and 1991 but showed a declining trend for the rest of the period. Inflow, of course, is not equivalent to immigration in so far as there is outflow as well. But the available data for a group of six Western European countries for the same period show that annual inflow and annual net immigration move together, i.e., the observed trends in the annual inflow are good indicators of the unobserved trends in annual immigration.[14]

Globalization, therefore, seems to have been associated with declining migratory flow between developing and industrialized countries. This, it may be thought, indicates that immigration policies in industrialized countries had become increasingly restrictive during the period. While this may indeed be

[14] See Ghose (2002), figure 4, p. 13.

Table 5.2 Annual inflow (in thousands) of legal immigrants from developing countries, 1988–98

	WE7	United States	Others
1988	149.5	439.1	n.a.
1989	169.8	822.5	322.1
1990	195.8	1 196.3	330.8
1991	193.6	1 476.5	392.1
1992	174.3	650.0	418.6
1993	161.1	577.2	371.3
1994	133.3	505.2	347.6
1995	127.6	465.4	308.1
1996	130.8	614.9	338.9
1997	135.5	553.1	370.6
1998	146.7	548.6	313.1

Note: WE7 denotes seven countries of Western Europe for which data are available. The countries are: Belgium, France, Germany, Netherlands, Norway, Sweden and Switzerland. Others include Australia, Canada and Japan.
n.a. = not available.

Source: Ghose (forthcoming).

so,[15] there are also reasons to think that the overall migratory pressure (and not just legal immigration) was actually declining during the period. We can get a rough measure of the overall migratory pressure by considering, in addition to legal immigrants, asylum seekers and clandestine immigrants. And we can ask the question: What would have been the trend in immigration during the 1990s had governments granted legal status to all asylum seekers and clandestine immigrants?

For the United States and the seven Western European countries represented in table 5.2, annual data on the number of asylum seekers from developing countries are also available. These data are used to construct table 5.3, which shows what the trends in immigration would have been had all asylum seekers been granted the status of legal immigrants. That the trends would not have been any different from the trends in legal immigration is immediately obvious

[15] Ghose (2002) shows that legal immigration into industrialized countries during 1988–98 was determined, to a large extent, by the interaction of a political compulsion to restrict immigration (arising from popular concerns about the social consequences of immigration) and an economic compulsion to allow immigration (arising from an extremely low rate of growth of the native labour force). It can be deduced from this that the recent growth of popular concerns has had the effect of reducing legal immigration.

Table 5.3 Annual inflow (in thousands) of foreign population (legal immigrants + asylum seekers) from developing countries, 1990–98

	WE7	United States
1990	326.7	n.a.
1991	329.6	1 568.4
1992	278.7	726.1
1993	274.5	683.0
1994	243.5	611.8
1995	246.4	596.7
1996	238.1	728.2
1997	248.1	617.9
1998	252.9	n.a.

Note: See note to table 5.2 for the list of countries included in WE7.

n.a. = not available.

Source: Ghose (2002).

from a comparison of tables 5.2 and 5.3; annual immigration would still have peaked in 1991 and declined thereafter.

We cannot directly show how the trends would have changed had the clandestine immigrants also been treated as legal immigrants. Firm estimates of annual inflow of clandestine immigrants are simply not available. We can do a thought experiment, however. Assuming that clandestine immigration from developing countries was zero (or any arbitrary number) in 1991, we can ask: If the annual inflow of foreign population (from developing countries) were to remain at the level reached in 1991, what would be the required annual inflow of clandestine immigrants from developing countries? The estimated figures, derived from the numbers in table 5.3, stand at around 0.08 million for the seven West European countries and around 0.9 million for the United States. These numbers seem improbably large when compared to the rough estimates of clandestine immigration that are available. Between 1992 and 1998, the number of clandestine immigrants into the European Union (15 Western European countries) from the rest of the world is estimated to have increased by around 1.3 million or by 0.2 million per annum.[16] And between 1992 and 1996, the number of clandestine immigrants into the United States from the rest of the world is estimated to have increased by 1.6 million or by 0.4 million per

[16] See World Bank (2001), p. 80.

annum.[17] So, even if all clandestine immigrants were offered legal status, the annual level of immigration would still have shown a declining trend after 1991.

We conclude that the overall migratory pressure was declining, not rising, during the period of globalization. This finding is not at odds with our theoretical expectation; the mainstream trade theory predicts that increased trade could either increase or reduce migratory pressures. What does seem surprising is that factors other than trade have apparently been inconsequential; migratory pressures declined in spite of the declining migration costs (as a result of declining costs of transportation and communication), the growing income gap between the richest and the poorest countries of the world (as noted in Chapter 3) and the increasing availability of information that characterized the 1990s. The explanation lies in the fact that, in the real world, these factors influence migration (legal or clandestine) of low-skilled workers and this type of migration tends to be confined to geographically proximate countries. We shall see below that most of the legal low-skilled immigrants in the United States are from Mexico and a few other countries of Central America. And there is evidence to show that in the United States most of the clandestine immigrants, who are generally low skilled, are also from Mexico and other Central American countries.[18] It is well known, too, that most of the clandestine immigrants in Western Europe are from Turkey, North Africa and Eastern Europe. These facts tell us that separate investigations are required to understand how migratory pressures may have changed in the 1990s within each of these clusters. But declining migration costs, growing income gaps and growing information flows cannot really be expected to increase migration from poor countries that are geographically remote from the industrialized countries. In fact, the geographically remote poor countries are not and have never been important suppliers of migrant workers to industrialized countries.[19]

The phenomenon of brain drain

Brain drain refers to the fact that the average skill level of the emigrant workers (from developing to industrialized countries) tends to be much higher than that of the populations of their home countries. Migration, then, has the effect of augmenting the stock of human capital in industrialized countries and of

[17] See Solimano (2001), table 2.

[18] According to the estimates of the US Immigration and Naturalization Service, Mexico and the countries of Central America and the Caribbean together account for nearly 74 per cent of the illegal immigrants in the United States. See Solimano (2001), table 2.

[19] The exceptions to this rule are observed when colonial–historical linkages come into play. Thus the United Kingdom, France and Portugal, for example, have substantial numbers of migrants from their geographically remote and poor ex-colonies.

Table 5.4 Average years of education of legal emigrants to the United States and of resident population, 1990

Region	Emigrants	Residents
Asia–Pacific	14.03	6.27
Middle East and North Africa	13.47	5.89
Sub-Saharan Africa	14.62	5.70
Central America and the Caribbean	10.83	6.32
South America	12.94	6.64
All regions	12.04	6.27

Note: **Asia–Pacific** includes Bangladesh, Fiji, India, Indonesia, Iran, Republic of Korea, Malaysia, Pakistan, Papua New Guinea, Philippines, Sri Lanka and Thailand. **Middle East and North Africa** includes Algeria, Sudan, Syria, Tunisia and Turkey. **Sub-Saharan Africa** includes Benin, Cameroon, Central African Republic, Congo, Gambia, Ghana, Kenya, Lesotho, Malawi, Mali, Mauritius, Mozambique, Rwanda, Senegal, Sierra Leone, South Africa, Togo, Uganda, Zambia and Zimbabwe. **Central America and the Caribbean** includes Costa Rica, Dominican Republic, El Salvador, Guatemala, Guyana, Honduras, Jamaica, Mexico, Nicaragua, Panama and Trinidad and Tobago. **South America** includes Argentina, Bolivia, Brazil, Chile, Colombia, Ecuador, Paraguay, Peru, Uruguay and Venezuela.

Source: Ghose (2002).

depleting it in developing countries. Moreover, rather perversely, the cost of augmenting the stock of human capital in industrialized countries is in effect borne by developing countries.

That brain drain is a very general feature of migration today is clear from the data presented in table 5.4. These data show, for the year 1990, the average number of years of education for populations of major developing regions and for the emigrants from these regions to the United States. The average emigrant, according to these data, had received twice as many years of education as the average inhabitant. There are even some indications that the education gap between the average emigrant and the average inhabitant may have been higher for lower-income countries; it appears to have been higher for sub-Saharan Africa than for other regions, for example.

Because brain drain is a general feature of migration from developing countries, a high rate of emigration from a region is associated with a high rate of brain drain. This is quite clear from the data presented in table 5.5. However, sub-Saharan Africa (with a low rate of emigration and a high rate of brain drain) again stands out as an exception to the rule. Otherwise, at one end of the spectrum is the Asia–Pacific region with low rates of emigration and brain drain, and at the other end is the Central America and Caribbean region with high rates of emigration and brain drain.

Table 5.5 highlights the fact that while brain drain is a significant problem for all parts of the developing world, it is a particularly serious problem for two

Table 5.5 Rate of legal emigration (%) to the United States by education category, 1990

Region	Years of education			
	0–8	9–12	13 or more	All categories
Asia–Pacific	0.01	0.43	2.86	0.19
Middle East and North Africa	0.01	1.04	2.10	0.18
Sub-Saharan Africa	0.00	0.20	6.89	0.10
Central America and Caribbean	1.10	33.45	17.98	7.38
South America	0.01	1.38	2.58	0.41
All regions	0.07	2.59	5.10	0.66

Note: For the list of countries in each region, see note to table 5.4.

Source: Ghose (2002).

regions – Central America and the Caribbean, and sub-Saharan Africa. Indeed, for certain countries of these regions, brain drain seems to be of truly astonishing magnitudes. To give some examples, the percentage of people with 13 or more years of education migrating was 58 for the Gambia, 33 for Mali, 25 for Sierra Leone, 47 for El Salvador, 81 for Guyana, 69 for Jamaica and 44 for Trinidad and Tobago.[20] And here we are considering emigration to the United States alone.

Table 5.5 also highlights another important fact. The rate of emigration of people with lower than tertiary level education is quite insignificant except for the Central America and Caribbean region, which accounted for 76 per cent of all emigrants with up to twelve years of education. Even for the Central America and Caribbean region, however, the rate of emigration of those with up to eight years of education is quite insignificant. These facts show that, first, cross-border migration of unskilled workers is negligible and, second, that geographical proximity is an important, perhaps the most important, determinant of cross-border migration of low-skilled workers.[21] It is quite clear that, for most of the developing countries, international migration is of no help in coping with the major labour market problem – that of surplus unskilled or low-skilled labour.[22]

[20] See Ghose (2002), table 6, p. 20. An important point that these facts suggest is that geographical proximity is not an important determinant of migration of skilled labour.

[21] It is now clear why the overall rate of emigration is not the sole determinant of the rate of brain drain. Geographical proximity is an important determinant of the former but not of the latter.

[22] This stands in sharp contrast to the fact that, during the nineteenth century globalization, emigration enabled several European countries to overcome the problem of surplus unskilled labour. In these countries, the labour force in 1910 was very substantially lower than it would have been but for the emigration during 1870–1910. See Appendix 5.1.

Though these data relate to migratory flows to the United States alone, the patterns revealed by them are most likely to hold for all migratory flows from developing to industrialized countries. The United States, as we have noted, is by far the most important destination for migrants from developing countries. And we have no good reason to think that data relating to migration to other industrialized countries, were they available, would have revealed quite different patterns.

One weakness of the data, however, is that they refer only to legal migration. They therefore understate the importance of emigration of low-skilled workers since clandestine migrants are mostly low skilled. But it should be evident from what has been said above that this can only be true for the Central America and Caribbean region, which, as mentioned in note 18, accounted for 74 per cent of all clandestine immigrants in the United States in 1990.

Was brain drain increasing in the 1990s? The observed declining rate of immigration into industrialized countries would imply a declining rate of brain drain if it can be assumed that the skill composition of immigrants remained unchanged. But trade theory leads us to expect precisely that the skill composition of immigrants changed in the 1990s, that the share of the high skilled increased and that of the low skilled correspondingly declined. There is some evidence that supports the proposition, though the evidence is only suggestive rather than conclusive. First, in many countries of the Organisation for Economic Co-operation and Development (OECD) there is excess demand for skilled labour. Second, most of the OECD countries have amended their immigration laws with a view to encouraging immigration of skilled workers; several have introduced special fast-track procedures for issuing immigration and work permits to highly skilled foreigners.[23] One study of immigration into the United States shows that the average education/skill level of new immigrants has been rising since the mid-1980s and that this is attributable, at least in part, to the changes in immigration laws.[24] Finally, there is evidence to show that a growing proportion of students from developing countries, pursuing higher education in OECD countries, has been staying on to work in these countries, presumably because the acquisition of work and stay permits has become progressively easier. Surveys carried out by the National Science Foundation show, for example, that the "stay rate" for such students in the United States increased from 50 per cent in 1985 to 80 per cent in 2000.[25]

[23] See OECD (2001), Ch. 5, for a fairly detailed account of the recent changes in immigration policies in industrialized countries.

[24] See Jasso, Rosenzweig and Smith (1998).

[25] See Devan and Tewari (2001).

International migration, then and now

It is by now well known that massive international migration occurred during the nineteenth century globalization. Between 1820 and 1920, about 60 million Europeans migrated to the New World (Argentina, Australia, Brazil, Canada and the United States). Annual emigration averaged 0.3 million between 1846 and 1876, over 0.6 million between 1876 and 1896, and over 1 million thereafter. These facts have led many economists to presume that the current process of globalization must also call for substantial growth of international migration. We have argued above that there is neither any theoretical reason nor any empirical evidence to suggest that the current process of globalization must necessarily increase migratory pressures. This creates a new puzzle. How is the massive international migration of the nineteenth century to be explained?

An explanation begins to emerge when we go beyond headcounts and look at the patterns. Three particular facts stand out. First, in the nineteenth century, both capital and labour migrated from Europe to the New World. This seems odd since it suggests that Europe had both surplus capital and surplus labour.[26] In today's world, labour abundance is synonymous with capital scarcity, and capital and labour generally move in opposite directions. Second, labour that migrated from Europe was largely unskilled or low skilled. There is even evidence to suggest that the skill level of the average European emigrant was declining over time. The large-scale emigration of low-skilled labour arguably facilitated the economic transformation of several European countries by drastically reducing their stocks of surplus labour.[27] The contrast with today's migration from the developing world is stark. Finally, at the time, Europe was economically more advanced than the New World. This means that labour was actually moving from more developed to less developed countries. Again, this is in marked contrast to today's pattern of international migration.

These contrasts are linked to another contrast: that relating to the nature of trade expansion. As noted in Chapter 2, in the nineteenth century it was trade in primary commodities (agricultural goods and minerals) that was expanding. In the course of the current process of globalization, it is trade in manufactures that has been expanding.

What these contrasts suggest is that the currently mainstream trade theory is not appropriate for explaining the nineteenth century trade between Europe and the New World. Indeed, the fact that the primary commodities are land-intensive

[26] Even at the time, the phenomenon appeared as odd to some economists. Hobson argued, for example, that the fact that Britain was exporting capital while British workers migrated or remained unemployed implied under-consumption in Britain, which resulted from the dominant ideology of "thrift as virtue" and the hugely unequal distribution of wealth. Malthus held somewhat similar views. See Keynes (1973), Ch. 23, and O'Rourke and Williamson (1999), p. 230, for discussions of these views.

[27] See Appendix 5.1.

(while manufactures are not) indicates that the trade theory appropriate for explaining nineteenth century trade is what economists refer to as the "specific factor model".

Schematically, the basis for trade in this framework is also traced to differences in factor endowments, but one of the countries (Country 1, say) is assumed to have abundant supplies of an inherently immobile specific factor (required to produce only certain types of goods), which we may take to be land. The other country (Country 2) can be assumed to have relatively abundant supplies of two mobile non-specific factors (required to produce all goods), capital and labour. Relative incomes of capital and labour, naturally, are higher in Country 1, while the relative income (rent) of land is higher in Country 2. Thus, on the one hand, there are incentives for capital and labour to move from Country 2 to Country 1. On the other hand, such movements are in fact required for trade between the two countries to expand. Obviously, Country 1 can profitably export land-intensive goods, while Country 2 can profitably export goods that are intensive in capital and labour; in other words, Country 1 will export primary commodities and Country 2 will export manufactures. Growth of trade will require production to rise in both countries. Growth of production in Country 1, however, will require increased supplies of the non-specific factors, and the required increased supplies will come from Country 2.

Within this framework, it is easy to see why large-scale international migration was a central feature of the nineteenth century globalization. But it is also clear why we cannot use that fact to predict that globalization today must also warrant increased international migration.

Conclusions

Trade and migration are not generally viewed as interlinked. In public debates on globalization, too, issues of international migration have not as yet figured prominently. However, economists tend to think that, in the absence of restrictive immigration laws, the recent growth of trade would have been associated with growth of international labour mobility just as it was in the course of the nineteenth century globalization.

In reality, the growth of trade seems to have reduced rather than increased migratory pressures. And this means that the restrictive immigration policies of industrialized countries have effectively served to create or aggravate the problem of clandestine immigration, mainly of low-skilled labour.

The available empirical evidence shows, at the same time, that South–North migration in today's world can be equated with brain drain from the South. And brain drain, it seems, has been growing. The empirical evidence, though inadequate, indicates this fairly strongly. Theoretical reasoning also suggests complementarities between North–South trade in manufactures and brain drain from the South. The recent changes in immigration policies of OECD countries, designed to encourage immigration of skilled labour only, points in the same direction.

Thus there are reasons to worry that many developing countries will find it hard to accumulate human capital and that this will undermine their long-term growth prospects. At the same time, for the majority of the developing countries, international migration leaves their most pressing labour market problem – that of surplus unskilled labour – unaffected. International migration today cannot do for developing countries what it did for Europe in the nineteenth century.

Appendix 5.1

Cumulative effects of emigration on population and labour force in European countries, 1870–1910

	Population	Labour force
Denmark	–11	–14
France	0	–1
Germany	–3	–4
Great Britain	–9	–11
Ireland	–36	–45
Italy	–31	–39
Netherlands	–2	–3
Norway	–19	–24
Portugal	–4	–5
Spain	–5	–6
Sweden	–15	–20

Note: Figures are estimated by using the formula: $(X–X^*)/X^*$, where X is the actual population or labour force in 1910 and X^* is an estimate of what the population or the labour force would have been in 1910 in the absence of emigration. The results are expressed as percentages. Thus Sweden's labour force in 1910 was 20 per cent below what it would have been in the absence of emigration.

Source: O'Rourke and Williamson (1999), p. 155.

TRADE AND LABOUR STANDARDS 6

Introduction

There is some anxiety in industrialized countries that the growing trade with low-income developing countries, where labour standards are naturally much lower, is undermining the high labour standards of their own countries. There is much talk of "unfair trade", "social dumping" and "race to the bottom". And there are demands for a variety of measures, particularly trade sanctions, to force improvement of labour standards in low-income countries.[1]

These concerns and demands, widespread though they are, remain rather vaguely formulated; and this makes it difficult to assess their empirical basis. It is quite unclear, for example, if the concern is about overall labour standards, about labour standards in particular industries or about standards relating to particular segments of the workforce. Terms such as "unfair trade", "social dumping" and "race to the bottom" tend to be used without much attention to their precise meanings or definitions. It is certainly not self-evident why North–South trade should undermine labour standards in the North today, while (presumably) it did not do so in the past.[2] And the basis for the belief that applying pressure on governments through trade sanctions can achieve quick improvement of labour standards in the South remains unexplained.

It is not surprising, therefore, that the concerns and demands are not backed by much more than anecdotal evidence; rigorous empirical work requires clearly defined issues and hypotheses. We have not analysed empirically the

[1] Sometimes the concern has a wider, humanitarian focus, reflecting a newly acquired awareness of the low labour standards prevailing in developing countries. But even those who adopt a global humanitarian perspective believe that the remedy lies in applying pressure on governments (or on multinational corporations involved in export-oriented production in developing countries) to improve labour standards. It should be said that the labour standards referred to in this context are "core" ILO standards relating to the freedom of association, the right to collective bargaining, and the elimination of child labour, forced labour and discrimination in employment.

[2] Neither North–South trade nor low labour standards in the South are novel phenomena. And labour standards in the developing world are generally better today than they were (say) 30 years ago.

effects of trade on labour standards in any of the preceding chapters, nor are we about to embark on such analysis in this chapter. Our objective here is not to report new findings or fresh policy proposals. The analysis presented below simply takes a serious look at the issues, assumptions and hypotheses that lie hidden in the popular concerns and demands.[3] Wherever relevant, we return to our empirical findings relating to the effects of trade on employment and wages to consider their implications for the issues at hand.

Trade and labour standards: Theory and evidence

Some preliminaries

It is useful to start by recognizing a basic fact: it is not the growth of trade as such but the growth of two-way trade in manufactures between industrialized and developing countries that provides the backdrop for the current debates on the linkage between trade and labour standards. This fact helps us to understand why these debates are occurring only now. Prior to the current globalization, North–South trade was overwhelmingly in non-competing products; the North exported manufactures to the South, while the South exported primary commodities to the North. This pattern ensured competition among the countries of the North on the one hand and among the countries of the South on the other. Competition among countries or enterprises always implies competition among workers. When German pharmaceutical companies were competing with American pharmaceutical companies for markets in developing countries, German workers were competing with American workers. Similarly, when Indian tea producers were competing with Sri Lankan tea producers for markets in industrialized countries, Indian workers were competing with Sri Lankan workers. International competition among workers is as old as international trade itself. But the older pattern of North–South trade created separate spheres of competition for Northern and Southern workers.[4] The really new element that globalization has introduced is North–South trade in competing products and this means that some workers in the North are now in competition with some workers in the South. It is this new kind of competition that has generated some new adjustment problems in Northern labour markets.[5]

---

[3] There are a number of recent studies that provide somewhat similar analyses. They also provide good surveys of the issues, the arguments and the evidence that have figured prominently in the literature. See, in particular, Maskus (1997); OECD (2000); Singh and Zammit (2000); Lee (1997); and Brown (2001).

[4] Competition among the workers of the globally excluded countries still occurs in a separate sphere, and the issues of labour standards in those countries do not figure in the current debates on trade and labour standards.

[5] Rodrik (1997, p. 5) points to this when he writes, "As the technology for manufactured goods becomes standardized and diffused internationally, nations with very different sets of values, norms, institutions, and collective preferences begin to compete head on in markets for similar goods. And the spread of globalization creates opportunities for trade between countries at very different levels of development."

From this viewpoint, it is easy to see why North–South trade is only now perceived as threatening to undermine the labour standards in the North. The new adjustment problems that underlie this perception are real and certainly deserve serious investigation. But it is important to recognize that the concern about the adjustment problems generated by North–South trade in competing products is quite distinct from the far more general concern about low labour standards in developing countries. It is not the case that low labour standards in the South are fine so long as North–South trade is not in competing products. Nor is it the case that labour standards in manufactures-exporting developing countries today are lower than those in the globally excluded developing countries (whose trade with the industrialized countries continues to be in non-competing products). In the current debates on the linkage between trade and labour standards, these simple facts often go unrecognized. This creates two seriously misleading impressions: first, that the low labour standards in the globally excluded countries are of no particular concern to the international community; and, second, that the concern about the adjustment problems in Northern labour markets is simultaneously a global humanitarian concern about the low labour standards in the manufactures-exporting developing countries.

In considering the linkage between trade and labour standards, the central question that we need to address is: Are there good reasons to believe that the growth of two-way trade in manufactures between industrialized and developing countries might be undermining the labour standards in industrialized countries, and perhaps even generally through a "race to the bottom"? This obviously is an important question. But we must be clear that this is quite different from questions of whether labour standards in developing countries are inappropriately low or of how to improve labour standards in developing countries in general.

An analytical perspective

We start by restating the basic trade-theoretic framework, outlined in Chapter 3, in the form of a simple illustrative example. Assume that there are only two products – machinery and textiles – that are produced in both North and South under autarky. Assume also (a) that the production of machinery is more skill-intensive than the production of textiles (correspondingly, textile production is more unskilled-labour-intensive than machinery production) in both North and South; (b) that, in both North and South, labour standards are higher in machinery production than in textile production; and (c) that labour standards are generally higher in the more developed North than in the less developed South.[6]

[6] This means that machinery workers in the North enjoy higher labour standards than machinery workers in the South, just as textile workers in the North enjoy higher labour standards than textile workers in the South.

When trade occurs, the North specializes in machinery production and the South specializes in textile production. As a result, the production and prices of machinery rise in the North and the production and prices of textiles rise in the South; correspondingly, the production and prices of textiles fall in the North and the production and prices of machinery fall in the South. So textile workers move to machinery production in the North and machinery workers move to textile production in the South. What happens to labour standards? There are two answers to the question. The first is that global labour standards worsen in textile production (because production is shifted to the South where labour standards are lower) and improve in machinery production (because production is shifted to the North where labour standards are higher). The second answer relates to changes in average labour standards within individual economies. In the North, average labour standards improve because textile workers move to machinery production and because standards in machinery production themselves rise in consequence of the price rise. The change is ambiguous in the South. On the one hand, labour standards improve in textile production in consequence of the price rise; on the other hand, the workers who move from machinery production to textile production suffer a decline in standards. The net effect depends on the numbers involved. As it is quite reasonable to suppose that the number of workers who were already in textile production is much larger than the number that moves in, it is quite likely that average labour standards improve in the South as well.

The simple trade-theoretic framework thus yields two hypotheses.[7] First, North–South trade in competing products inevitably leads to an improvement in global standards in those industries in which the North has a comparative advantage and to a lowering of global standards in those industries in which the South has a comparative advantage. At a global level, therefore, there is a widening of the "standards gap" between industries. Second, in consequence of North–South trade in competing products, the average labour standards improve in the North and are quite likely to improve in the South as well.

An important point that these hypotheses bring to attention is that, in discussing the linkage between trade and labour standards, it is necessary to specify if the reference is to global standards in individual industries or to average standards in individual countries. If the concern is about erosion of

[7] The illustrative example is constructed on the assumption that, once trade occurs, there is complete specialization in production. This, of course, need not happen; both products can continue to be produced in both countries. But so long as machinery production expands and textile production contracts in the North and the opposite happens in the South, the hypotheses remain unaltered. The basic trade-theoretic framework also assumes full employment under autarky and smooth labour market adjustments in the course of transition to openness. These assumptions are obviously unrealistic, but their abandonment does not invalidate the prediction that machinery production will expand in the North and contract in the South while textile production will contract in the North and expand in the South.

global standards in certain industries, those in which the South is specializing, then it is unquestionably well founded. But such a concern can be addressed only by imposing a ban on North–South trade in competing products. Few would consider this as a serious option.

The appropriate question to consider is the following. Does the available empirical evidence support the hypothesis that North–South trade in competing products improves average labour standards in both North and South? Much further research is required for a satisfactory answer to emerge. But the research results reported in Chapter 4 allow us to provide a tentative answer.

Labour standards can be judged by a combination of two indicators: real wages (which indicate the level of welfare of worker households) and non-wage benefits (which are benefits derived from the physical environment at the workplace, standards of occupational safety and health, regulations concerning working hours, job security provisions, social security arrangements, collective bargaining institutions and so forth). Empirical evidence on real wages, of course, is far more easily available than that on non-wage benefits. However, it is hard to find instances where rising real wages are associated with declining non-wage benefits; it can be plausibly assumed that when real wages rise, non-wage benefits either rise or remain unchanged but do not decline. Thus, growth of real wages can be regarded as a fairly good indicator of changes in labour standards.

Our evidence is that since the early 1980s real wage growth in manufacturing has been significant in both industrialized and manufactures-exporting developing countries, and for both skilled and unskilled workers. In the industrialized countries, the share of high-skill jobs in total manufacturing employment has also increased so that there has been an unambiguous increase in non-wage benefits as well. Thus there has been an unambiguous improvement in labour standards in manufacturing industries. However, the changes in the manufactures-exporting developing countries have been more complex. In most of these countries (in China, India, Malaysia and Mexico in our sample), the growth of real wages has been associated with a change in the composition of manufacturing employment; the share of the regulated sector jobs in total manufacturing employment has tended to decline. This makes the change in average labour standards ambiguous, since some erosion of average non-wage benefits has accompanied the real wage growth. In some other countries (in Brazil in our sample), however, the share of high-skill jobs in total manufacturing employment has risen so that the average labour standards in manufacturing have unambiguously improved.

Thus neither theory nor the available evidence supports the idea that the growing trade with low-income developing countries has been eroding labour standards in industrialized countries. The average labour standards in manufacturing, the sector directly affected by trade with developing countries, seem to have improved, as theory leads us to expect. This does not, of course, imply that economy-wide labour standards have also improved; but it does imply that if they have deteriorated, the reason is not growing trade with developing countries in competing products.

This conclusion would surprise many who believe that North–South trade erodes labour standards in the North. But the surprise, though understandable, is unwarranted for the following reasons. In the first place, improvement in average labour standards does not preclude the possibility of worsened standards for some workers. Even the simple trade-theoretic framework suggests that the redundant textile workers in the North would be re-employed in machinery production only at a lower wage, and the higher non-wage benefits in machinery production may or may not compensate for this. Thus judgements can vary depending upon whether we focus on average standards for all workers or on standards for only a specific section of workers. There is often an implicit emphasis on the fact that some workers are adversely affected, while ignoring the fact that a majority of the workers are favourably affected at the same time.

It is to be noted, secondly, that the possibility that a movement from less to more trade openness may involve changes in the level of employment has not even been considered in our analysis here. The reason is that labour standards, by definition, refer only to the qualitative dimensions of employment and hence are not affected by changes in the quantity of employment (the evidence on which has been examined in detail in Chapter 4). In popular perceptions, however, changes in the quantity of employment tend to become indistinguishable from changes in labour standards.

The nature of the relationship between changes in labour standards and changes in employment should, of course, be regarded as an important issue. But this is a separate issue, which we address below (in the context of developing countries only).

"Unfair trade" and "social dumping"

People in industrialized countries observe that some apparently efficient producers in their own countries fail to withstand competition from producers in developing countries. It appears to them that since the reason for this failure does not lie in any inefficiency of the producers in their own countries, it must lie in the "unfair" cost advantage that producers in developing countries allegedly derive from the much lower labour standards prevailing there. Some of the job losses in industrialized countries, it thus seems to them, occur because of the "unfair" competition that trade with developing countries entails.

A little reflection tells us that the common notion of unfair trade is based on two incorrect assumptions. The first is that absolute cost advantage counts in trade. The basic insight provided by the theory of comparative advantage is precisely that absolute costs are of little consequence; trade occurs between two countries even when one of them has absolute cost advantage in all lines of production. Even if the developing country producers derived any cost advantage from the low labour standards, this could not be the reason for their trade success. If the textile producers in the United States are competed out of existence by the textile producers in China, then this is not because the Chinese textile producers are more "efficient" (i.e., have lower absolute costs of production) than the American textile producers but because the Chinese textile producers are relatively more "efficient" than the Chinese producers of computers, while the American textile producers are relatively less "efficient" than the American producers of computers. The second incorrect assumption is that lower labour standards necessarily imply a lower unit cost of labour. In fact, low labour standards generally reflect a low level of labour productivity so that they do not usually imply a low unit labour cost. Indeed, it is often the case that countries with lower labour standards have higher unit labour costs than countries with higher labour standards. Studies have shown that cross-country variation in wages is almost wholly explained by the cross-country variation in labour productivity so that there is little systematic cross-country variation in the unit labour cost.[8]

The popular notion of social dumping also arises from an incorrect understanding of the notion of dumping. According to the standard definition, dumping occurs when, for any given product, a producer charges a lower price in the export market than in the domestic market. Correspondingly, social dumping can be accurately said to occur if, for example, a garment producer in Bangladesh pays lower wages to workers producing garments for export to the United States than it pays to workers producing garments for sale in Bangladesh. There is no evidence to show that this happens in Bangladesh or anywhere else in the world. If anything, the evidence actually shows that export-oriented units, particularly those located in export processing zones, pay higher wages and offer better working conditions than other units producing similar products for domestic markets.[9]

The point is not that cases of unfair trade or social dumping may not arise. The point is that in order to argue that such cases are rampant in the context of North–South trade in manufactures, it is necessary to demonstrate (i) that, in the context of North–South trade, a lower unit labour cost can be an advantage;

[8] See Golub (1999); Rodrik (1999); and Kucera (2001), for example.

[9] See, for example, Moran (2002); ILO (1998); and Oxfam (2002).

(ii) that lower labour standards imply lower unit labour costs; and (iii) that producers in developing countries maintain lower labour standards in production for export than in production for the domestic market. The existing literature provides no basis for supposing that these propositions have empirical validity.[10]

"Race to the bottom"

From what has been said above, it should already be clear that if race to the bottom is interpreted to mean dilution of labour standards in industrialized countries in consequence of trade with developing countries, then there is no empirical ground for arguing that globalization has induced such a thing. Nobody suggests that the traditional North–South trade in non-competing products undermines labour standards in the North. And, as we have seen, there is neither any theoretical reason nor any empirical basis for supposing that trade in competing products with developing countries undermines labour standards in industrialized countries.

Race to the bottom could alternatively be interpreted to mean that developing countries, in their eagerness to expand manufactured exports and to attract foreign capital, might end up further lowering their already low labour standards. But there are no good reasons to think that a race to the bottom in this sense is under way. There is no clear evidence to show that expanding trade has undermined labour standards in manufactures-exporting developing countries. Nor is there evidence to suggest that countries with low labour standards have better export performance than those with high labour standards or that foreign investors favour countries with lower labour standards.[11] In short, empirically, no signs of a race to the bottom of the type in question have so far been detected. Even in theory, low labour standards can affect comparative advantage if and only if they are associated with high labour productivity, an association that is not found in reality. And low labour standards can be attractive to foreign investors if and only if they coexist with good physical and social infrastructure, a coexistence that is also not found in reality.

A third way of interpreting race to the bottom is to recognize that competition among exporters of primary commodities to industrialized countries can cause a fall in international prices of primary commodities.

[10] Rodrik (1997) defends the notion of unfair trade by arguing that "trade has implications for domestic norms and social arrangements and that its legitimacy rests in part on its compatibility with these" (p. 37). But it is hard to think of economic changes that meet this criterion of legitimacy. In fact, economic changes generally require adjustments in "norms and social arrangements" and there is no reason why we should rule out such adjustments if and when they become necessary because of changes in trade policy. Developing countries are routinely advised by international organizations as well as by well-known economists to make precisely such adjustments.

[11] See OECD (1996, 2000); Brown (2001); and Kucera (2001).

Falling international prices, in turn, could lead to a fall in real wages (and hence a deterioration of labour standards) in the commodity-producing sectors of the exporting countries. Moreover, falling commodity prices, through their adverse effects on economic growth, could have a generally negative effect on incomes of all workers. Thus, in the case of the countries dependent on exports of primary commodities, a competitive dilution of labour standards is possible.

Indeed, empirically, there are strong indications that a race to the bottom of this type has been under way for a fairly long time. Relative international prices of virtually all the primary commodities have declined sharply since 1980,[12] and a major reason has been persistent oversupply.[13] Evidence shows that, even in the face of declining prices, new exporters continue to emerge (in recent years, Indonesia has emerged as an exporter of cocoa and Viet Nam has emerged as an exporter of coffee) and old exporters continue to expand production, causing further decline in prices.[14] The only plausible explanation of these trends is that each individual country, faced with declining prices, tries to sustain its earnings by expanding its share of the export market and ends up reducing prices and earnings for all exporters. The gainers from this race to the bottom obviously are the major importing countries, i.e., the industrialized countries.

Race to the bottom is thus a reality, not just a possibility. It is linked not to the new kind of North–South trade in competing products but to the traditional North–South trade in non-competing products. It is a race confined to the group of exporters of primary commodities, the group of globally excluded countries.[15] It is a race that pre-dates globalization and explains, in large part, the phenomenon of global exclusion. And yet, this race to the bottom has neither aroused public concern nor attracted attention in the academic literature.

Improving labour standards in a developing economy

In much of the discussion on trade and labour standards, an implicit assumption is that governments can manipulate labour standards in much the same way as they can manipulate, say, tax or exchange rates. This assumption is made when,

---

[12] See UNCTAD (2002a); and World Bank (2002).

[13] See UNCTAD (2002a).

[14] For example, between 1997 and 2000, global coffee production increased by 21 per cent while the nominal price in international markets declined by 53 per cent. See World Bank (2002), p. 211.

[15] Direct evidence on trends in labour standards in the globally excluded countries is not easy to find. But there is much evidence of poor economic growth, deteriorating employment conditions and rising poverty in many of these countries, particularly in those of sub-Saharan Africa and Latin America, and these trends imply deteriorating labour standards. See Collier and Gunning (1999); ECLAC (2002); Chen and Ravallion (2001); Sala-i-Martin (2002); UNCTAD (2002a); and Oxfam (2002).

for example, it is argued that pressures on governments through trade sanctions or other means can bring about the immediate improvement of labour standards in developing countries.[16] The assumption is also made when it is argued that governments deliberately lower labour standards in order to increase exports or to attract FDI.[17] The idea underlying the assumption could only be that improving labour standards is a matter of introducing and enforcing appropriate regulations, a matter of political choice and administrative action. According to this view, it can be argued that low labour standards in developing countries reflect to a large extent the unwillingness of their governments to introduce and enforce such regulations. External pressures could then, arguably, turn this unwillingness into willingness and hence improve labour standards.[18]

If this proposition were valid, however, the very concern that trade with low-income countries erodes labour standards in industrialized countries would deserve to be dismissed without discussion. If governments are assumed to have the ability to manipulate labour standards through regulatory interventions alone, it is also legitimate to assume that this ability is substantially greater in the case of Northern governments than in the case of Southern governments. Any erosion of labour standards in industrialized countries, therefore, must fundamentally reflect the unwillingness of their governments to protect the standards and cannot be blamed on trade.[19] The argument that trade sanctions or any other form of external pressure on governments can improve labour standards in developing countries in the short run is logically inconsistent with the argument that trade erodes labour standards in industrialized countries.

But let us put this problem of logical consistency aside and focus on the proposition that governments in developing countries can bring about quick

[16] If the assumption is not made, the demand for trade sanctions as a cure for problems of low labour standards boils down to the proposition that labour standards in any given situation can be improved simply by destroying the low-quality jobs. For, if governments do not have the ability to improve labour standards at will, trade sanctions can only destroy the allegedly low-quality jobs in export industries.

[17] This argument is in fact difficult to understand. If low labour standards do not mean low unit labour costs, as we have argued above, governments' attempts (in so far as such attempts do occur in reality) to gain advantage in trade or in attracting foreign investment by lowering labour standards can only be attributed to ignorance. It is hard to believe that governments in developing countries actually suffer from such ignorance. Here, however, we are interested in pursuing a different issue. Can any government actually lower labour standards even if it wants to? And even if it could do so, what ensures the desired labour supply?

[18] Popular opinion in industrialized countries often favours applying pressures (through boycott of products or of shares in stock markets) on the multinational corporations that are engaged in export-oriented production in developing countries. Such pressures can conceivably lead to improvements in labour standards in the production units directly managed by these corporations; indeed, there are instances where this has happened. But, as our subsequent discussion will make clear, it is by no means certain that this results in an improvement in average labour standards in the countries concerned.

[19] Freeman (1994, p. 87) argues precisely this: "... I do not accept the premise of some that bad standards drive out good standards. Any country that wants higher labour standards can have them ... if it is willing to pay. A country can pay for standards that increase its cost of production in three ways: through exchange rate devaluation, with all consumers bearing the burden; through lower wages of workers who gain the benefits; or through taxes on the general public." He is, of course, referring to industrialized countries.

improvement in labour standards through the introduction and enforcement of appropriate regulations alone. A little reflection tells us that such a proposition can be taken seriously only if we think in terms of improving labour standards for a particular segment of the workforce (say, for workers in export industries) in any given country. For, even if it were in principle possible to improve labour standards for the entire workforce merely through regulatory interventions, and even if there were no lack of political will, developing country governments would still not be in a position to achieve the improvement in the short run because of the constraints imposed by limitations of administrative capacity and of resources to meet the required enforcement costs.

Supposing we assume away such constraints, is it then reasonable to argue that the average labour standards for the entire workforce in any given developing country can be improved merely through regulatory interventions? The answer is no, since we cannot assume that problems of labour standards have nothing to do with problems of employment structure, unemployment, underemployment and poverty that are typically associated with low level of development. We only have to recall the stylized account of the dualistic labour market (presented in Chapter 4), typical of developing countries, to realize this. In situations where regular (full-time) wage employment is not the dominant form of employment and where desperately poor people are looking for just any kind of job, regulatory interventions by even omnipotent governments cannot possibly ensure desirable labour standards for all workers.

An illustrative example is perhaps helpful. Consider the situation prevailing in India, a country that can be regarded as relatively advanced (among low-income developing countries) and where there is a long tradition of regulatory interventions designed to ensure minimum labour standards. Just around 50 per cent of the workers in India are wage employees, the other 50 per cent being self-employed (including unpaid family workers). Of the wage employees, roughly 10 per cent have regular jobs in what we define as the regulated sector; another 20 per cent have regular jobs outside the regulated sector; and the remaining 70 per cent work as casual labourers (searching for jobs on a daily basis and, if and when successful, earning a daily wage). There is evidence to show that the regular wage employees, irrespective of whether they are in or outside the regulated sector, earn above-poverty-line incomes though, of course, regular employees in the regulated sector earn substantially higher incomes than those outside. On the other hand, a large majority of the casual labourers and a sizeable section of the self-employed earn below-poverty-line incomes. Not surprisingly, the working conditions of these two groups of workers also reflect the lowest labour standards in the country.

In such a context, improving the average labour standards effectively means improving labour standards for the most disadvantaged groups of workers – the casual wage labourers and the self-employed with a poor asset base. Yet, regulatory interventions by successive governments have achieved very little in this regard, and it is not very difficult to understand why. It is not just that the problems of enforcement are huge. It is in fact hard to see what regulatory interventions could do for these categories of workers or even what the appropriate instruments of regulatory interventions might be.

On the other hand, it is fairly obvious that if it were possible to transfer these workers into regular wage employment even in the unregulated sector, absolute poverty would sharply decline and the average labour standards (for all workers) would rise. In other words, improving labour standards for the poorest section of the workforce requires a change in the structure of employment. And for such a change to occur, regular wage employment must grow at a rapid enough rate to make it possible to shift the poorest workers out of their current jobs into new regular jobs.[20] Measures that increase regular wage employment in the economy, therefore, are also measures that improve the average labour standards for all workers. By the same reasoning, measures that reduce regular wage employment in the economy are also measures that worsen the average labour standards for all workers.

The overall point to be derived from the illustrative example is that persistence of low labour standards in developing countries does not in general imply their governments' unwillingness to improve these standards. Regulatory interventions by governments, even in the best of circumstances, cannot improve the average labour standards for all workers in today's developing countries, where sizeable sections of the apparently employed workers are effectively unemployed without any social security support. One reason is that governments have limited administrative capacity and limited ability to meet the enforcement costs. A much more fundamental reason is that regulatory interventions are largely irrelevant for the poorest workers who form the majority of the workforce.

There still remains a question that can legitimately be asked. Should governments nevertheless use regulatory interventions to improve labour standards for even a small section of the regular employees? The answer would be in the affirmative only if such interventions do not adversely affect the growth of regular wage employment in the economy. This is where the question of the relationship between labour standards and employment assumes significance. If

[20] More concretely, the rate of growth of regular wage employment in the economy must be faster than the rate of growth of the labour force.

efforts to improve labour standards for a section of the regular wage employees through regulatory interventions cause a slowdown in the growth of regular wage employment in the economy, the consequence is a slowdown or a halt in the improvement of labour standards for the poorest sections of the workforce – the casual wage labourers and the self-employed with an extremely poor asset base. The possibility of such a trade-off between an improvement of conditions of those already in regular wage employment and an improvement in the conditions of those who are yet to be in regular wage employment cannot be ruled out *a priori*, though its nature and significance are likely to be situation specific and can be known only through investigative work.

It should be clear why trade sanctions (or any other form of pressure on governments) are unlikely to improve average labour standards for all workers in developing countries in the short run. Pressures on governments might conceivably improve labour standards for some workers, who are already in regular wage employment (and hence are among the relatively better-off), but the desirability of this is open to question if it has the effect of undermining the growth of regular wage employment.[21] On the other hand, since trade itself improves labour standards in so far as it stimulates the growth of regular wage employment, trade sanctions would deprive governments of an important instrument of intervention.

These insights enable us to view the observed effects of trade on labour standards in manufactures-exporting developing countries in a clearer perspective. In most of these countries, as we have seen, increased trade has had the effect of increasing regular wage employment in manufacturing industries. Moreover, the employment effect has been more significant for unskilled than for skilled labour. Thus, even though the change in the average labour standards for the regular wage employees in manufacturing industries has been somewhat ambiguous, there is little doubt that the average labour standards for the working population in the economy as a whole have improved.

Concluding remarks

The concern that trade in competing products (manufactures) with developing countries may be undermining labour standards in industrialized countries does not have a basis in either theoretical reasoning or empirical evidence. The

[21] It should also be clear at this point why pressures on multinational corporations (whose domain of action in any particular developing country is even more limited than that of the government) may not have the effect of improving average labour standards. At best, such pressures benefit only a tiny segment of the workforce. And there may be a cost in the form of a slowdown in the growth of regular wage employment, which hurts the prospects of the even poorer workers – the casual labourers and the self-employed.

common notions of unfair trade and social dumping, on close scrutiny, turn out to be based on incorrect assumptions. Race to the bottom is a reality, but the context is not North–South trade in manufactures; it is confined to the globally excluded countries, the countries that depend heavily on exports of primary commodities to industrialized countries. It means the competitive bidding-down of prices of primary commodities in international markets by the exporters of these commodities. This race to the bottom has its beneficiaries – the industrialized countries that are the major importers of primary commodities.

In addressing the more general concern about low labour standards in developing countries, it is important to recognize that low labour standards fundamentally reflect problems of surplus labour and undeveloped employment structure. These problems cannot be remedied merely through regulatory interventions by governments; what is required is growth of regular wage employment at a rate faster than that of the labour force. Policies that promote rapid growth of regular wage employment, therefore, are also policies that improve labour standards. It is in this sense that trade itself can be an instrument for improving labour standards in low-income countries. More generally, rapid growth of unskilled-labour-intensive modern manufacturing is required to improve labour standards in most developing countries.

Regulatory interventions, even in the best of circumstances, can only be effective in improving labour standards for a small section of the workers, a section that already is in regular wage employment and hence enjoys higher labour standards than the self-employed poor and the casual wage labourers. And, aside from some obvious questions of equity and fairness, such improvements may not even imply unambiguous social gain in all circumstances, for there may be trade-offs. Regulatory interventions to improve conditions of those who already are in regular wage employment may have the effect of slowing down the growth of regular wage employment in the economy, in which case there would be a slowdown of the process of improvement in labour standards for the poorest majority of the workers. For these reasons, the proposition that international pressures on governments can improve labour standards in low-income countries cannot be accepted as generally valid. And while it may well be valid in some specific cases, identification of such cases requires very careful empirical investigation.

CONCLUSIONS 7

Globalization has aroused widespread popular anxieties as well as intense academic debates. The issues involved relate largely, though not exclusively, to the perceived effects of globalization on employment, wages and incomes of people across the world. We have tried to assess these effects empirically in this book. Our analysis shows that many of the popular anxieties are not in fact well founded. At the same time, there are developments that ought to cause concern but have not actually attracted attention. The academic debates, on the other hand, have remained mostly inconclusive, partly because they have been far too focused on the problems faced by the advanced industrialized countries, while a global view is what is required. And an atmosphere of polarization between the proponents and the opponents of free trade has not helped; there is no need to view globalization as presenting us with a stark choice between free trade and autarky.

Globalization is often thought to have increased global income inequality. Our analysis shows that there is no sound empirical basis for such an assertion. In the first place, global income inequality can be shown to have increased since the early 1980s only if inequality is interpreted as the gap in per capita GDP between the richest and the poorest countries of the world. However, this measure also indicates that global income inequality has been rising since the early part of the nineteenth century. Besides, the empirical evidence does not show that the rise in this type of inequality since the early 1980s can be attributed to the widespread trade liberalization. The evidence does show, on the other hand, that freer trade has contributed to a reduction, for the first time in history, in the inequality of the distribution of per capita GDP among the world's population. The underlying reason is that freer trade has enabled a number of populous low-income developing countries to grow significantly faster than the high-income industrialized countries.[1]

[1] There is evidence to show that the within-country income inequality increased in many countries in the last two decades of the twentieth century. Nevertheless, the inequality of *world income distribution* showed a declining trend, not dissimilar to that in the inequality of the distribution of per capita GDP among the world's population.

On the effects of globalization on jobs and wages, it has been commonplace to argue that globalization has generated costs for the industrialized countries without bringing benefits to the developing countries. Globalization, it is asserted, has been responsible for the growing labour market disadvantages for low-skilled labour and the rising wage inequality in the industrialized world. At the same time, it is alleged to have led to the growth of low-quality jobs in developing countries, contributing to declining labour standards and growing poverty. The available empirical evidence does not support these views.

Increased trade in manufactures with low-income developing countries has undoubtedly had an adverse effect on the demand for low-skilled labour in the manufacturing industries of the developed countries. But its quantitative significance is too small to explain the economy-wide changes in the employment conditions of low-skilled labour. In fact, skill-biased technological change, unrelated to trade, has had a more significant adverse effect on the demand for low-skilled labour. However, these changes can at best explain the declining demand for low-skilled labour in the manufacturing sector; they do not explain the economy-wide labour market disadvantages of the low skilled. Given that services account for the bulk of employment in the industrialized countries and that a process of labour transfer from manufacturing into services had got under way long before the onset of globalization, the economy-wide changes in the demand for low-skilled labour have to be explained in terms of the developments in the services sector. This is also where explanations for the increased differential between high-skilled and low-skilled labour have to be sought. The pattern of growth in real wages in manufacturing industries is explicable entirely in terms of the pattern of growth in labour productivity (this was faster in high-skill industries), which is in turn linked to the pattern of technological change. And while the inter-industry differentials in wages can be shown to have increased (because of growing inter-industry differentials in labour productivity), this by itself does not imply rising wage differentials between high-skilled and low-skilled labour within the manufacturing sector.[2]

On the other hand, there is little doubt that increased North–South manufactured trade has had a stimulating effect on the growth of manufacturing employment in a majority of the integrating developing economies. The stimulating effect, moreover, has been stronger for low-skill employment than for high-skill employment. It is true that the employment in export industries is generally of lower quality than that in import-competing industries; but this is

[2] Inter-industry wage differentials also increased in the integrating developing countries, and for similar reasons. Moreover, in both types of countries, industrialized and developing, the wage differentials grew in a context of generally rising real wages. Within the industrialized world, real wages and productivity in low-skill industries stagnated only in the United States.

hardly surprising since the import-competing industries are relatively high-skill industries developed in the pre-globalization period under autarkic import-substitution regimes. The important fact is that the employment in export industries is of higher quality than that in many non-traded industries which, together with agriculture, account for the bulk of the employment in these economies. And for the workers in export industries, this employment is of higher quality than the jobs they previously held. Undoubtedly, there is much scope for improving the quality of employment in export industries, but the same can be said of most of the existing jobs in these countries, which have dualistic labour markets and substantial stocks of surplus labour. The important point to consider is not the quality of employment in a particular segment of the economy at any given point of time but the time-trend in the average quality of employment in the economy as a whole. It cannot be doubted that export growth has increased the average quality of employment in these countries. This is also evident from the rising real wages and the declining incidence of poverty.

Globalization, it has been argued, has set a race to the bottom in motion. Again, the available empirical evidence provides no support to this argument. Real wages in manufacturing have been rising in virtually all integrating economies, industrialized and developing. Indeed, our analysis shows that trade affected wages only in so far as it stimulated growth of labour productivity, perhaps by facilitating international diffusion of technology and by intensifying competition in product markets. Be that as it may, it is most unlikely that the observed growth of real wages has been accompanied by falling labour standards. Thus there is really no evidence to suggest that expanding North–South trade in manufactures has led to a competitive dilution of labour standards in either North or South. Moreover, the available evidence does not suggest that countries with lower labour standards are more successful in exporting or in attracting FDI flows. And we find no convincing reasons to believe that manufactured trade between the industrialized and developing countries generally involves unfair competition or social dumping.

Curiously, while many of the popular anxieties turn out to be unfounded, there are, at the same time, worrying developments that have failed to attract adequate public attention. The first and foremost of these is the phenomenon of global exclusion. A large number of developing countries have become progressively marginal to the global economy since the onset of globalization. Nearly 30 per cent of the world's population lives in these globally excluded countries. While not all of the excluded countries are poor, virtually all the poorest countries (those categorized as least developed by the United Nations) are among the excluded. There is not much doubt that employment and labour standards have been declining in these countries.

Global exclusion is to a large extent attributable to the declining prices of primary commodities in international markets. The causes are complex. On the one hand, globalization has not had a stimulating effect on the global demand for primary commodities. The short-run explanation is that there has not been much progress towards liberalization of trade in these commodities; this is a well-recognized flaw in the globalization process. But there are also long-term factors such as low and declining income elasticity of demand for primary commodities. On the other hand, there has been a persistent race to the bottom – competitive lowering of commodity prices and hence of employment and labour standards – among the excluded countries. The problem manifests itself in the perverse supply response; in international markets, supplies of primary commodities tend to rise as prices fall.

Clearly, a solution to the problem of global exclusion has to be found, and this will require simultaneous actions on several fronts. Trade in primary commodities, particularly in agricultural commodities, ought to be liberalized to the same extent as the trade in manufactures. A mechanism has also to be found for stabilization of prices at levels that allow the exporting countries to sustain economic growth, increase employment and improve labour standards. Trade liberalization by itself cannot stabilize prices; it can stimulate demand in the short run but will do nothing to remedy the supply-side problem of race to the bottom. Moreover, substantially increased international assistance has to be offered to the least developed countries to enable them to diversify their exports in the medium term. For, even with liberalized trade and stable prices, the world demand for primary commodities is most likely to continue to grow at a decelerating rate.

A second area of concern arises from the fact that trade liberalization has apparently promoted non-beneficial integration into the global economy for some developing countries. In the case of some countries from Latin America, although trade liberalization improved trade performance, better trade performance failed to improve growth performance. This, together with the fact that trade liberalization promoted inappropriate restructuring of manufacturing production, explains the rather unfavourable consequences of globalization for employment in these countries. These experiences suggest that liberalization programmes need to be designed with great care, taking due account of a country's specific macroeconomic context. Obviously, in negotiating global trade agreements it is virtually impossible to take account of each country's individual circumstances. But it is not impossible to identify certain broad categories of problems and to formulate trade liberalization strategies with these in view.

Indeed, what both the phenomenon of global exclusion and the experience of Latin American countries such as Brazil and Mexico underline is that trade liberalization had often been pursued as a goal in itself, without much concern about its consequences for economic growth and employment. Yet the goal is development, and trade liberalization is only an instrument that may or not be appropriate for particular countries. Future negotiations on trade agreements must reckon with the fact that trade liberalization does not promote trade or development in all circumstances.

Related to this is a third area of concern associated with global economic growth. Though we have not analysed this here, it is fairly well known that globalization has not had a stimulating effect on global economic growth. In fact, the rate of growth of world GDP has been decelerating since the mid-1960s; it was 5.1 per cent during 1965–74, 3.7 per cent during 1970–79, 2.9 per cent during 1975–84, 3.2 per cent during 1980–89, 2.8 per cent during 1985–94 and 2.5 per cent during 1990–99. Puzzling though the combination of globalization and decelerating global economic growth is, it has received scant attention in the literature and the explanations remain to be found. It cannot be doubted, however, that if the global economic growth continues to decelerate, world trade cannot continue to grow. Trade could thus become a zero-sum game: expansion of one country's trade would mean contraction of another's. Clearly, ways of stimulating global economic growth must be found. In a globalized world, this will require international cooperation on coordinated restructuring of monetary and fiscal policies that have by now become far too focused on inflation control and exchange rate management in both industrialized and developing countries.

A fourth area of concern relates to international labour mobility. Contrary to popular perceptions in the industrialized countries, South–North migration is mainly of skilled labour, and is more appropriately termed brain drain. There is some evidence to suggest that brain drain has been on the rise since the mid-1980s, and we can expect globalization to increase this trend. In the short run, brain drain means a substantial waste of scarce public resources invested in education in developing countries. In the long run, it means a widening of the already huge gap in human capital endowments between industrialized and developing countries. This can only increase global income inequality, as it will undermine the possibility for the developing countries to catch up with the industrialized countries.

There is an urgent need to think about a policy response at the international level to the problem of brain drain. Individual countries cannot find a solution that does not violate human rights; international cooperation is essential for designing a policy response that is beneficial for both South and North. International agreements on suitable compensation schemes and on migration regimes that permit only temporary, fixed-period migration for both unskilled and skilled labour are among the policy options that could be considered.

Our analysis suggests a fifth area of concern. Labour market policies in many of the industrialized countries do not seem to have been geared to addressing the problems arising from deindustrialization. The basic objective of labour market policies in these countries has been to promote flexibility, and there is some evidence to suggest that these policies have been responsible, to an extent, for the growing labour market disadvantages of low-skilled labour. The proper objective of labour market policies in the industrialized countries should be to facilitate labour transfer from manufacturing into services. Deindustrialization is a sign of dynamism in mature industrial economies. It pre-dates globalization, though arguably globalization has caused an acceleration of the process. And it calls for a restructuring of labour market institutions and skill development systems, because service industries differ quite substantially from manufacturing industries in terms of organizational characteristics and processes of technical change.

A sixth area of concern relates to labour market policies in the integrating developing economies. In the short run, these policies need to address the problems arising from what is called labour market churning. Even though manufacturing employment has been growing in most of these countries, there are parallel processes of job destruction and job creation. This means that, even in the most successfully integrating country, there are job losers who are in need of safety nets and assistance in job search. Labour market policies need to respond to these needs in the short run. The long-run objectives of labour market policies in these countries should be to facilitate transfer of labour from agriculture into manufacturing and to facilitate the transition from simple to progressively sophisticated manufacturing. Here there are questions of building appropriate labour market institutions and strategies for human resource development.

Finally, our findings argue against the use of trade sanctions for improving labour standards in low-income developing countries. As the public concerns about unfair competition, social dumping and race to the bottom within the group of integrating countries turn out to be unfounded, there is no general case for linking trade with labour standards. A race to the bottom is observed only in the case of the globally excluded countries, but trade sanctions obviously cannot cure the problem. In the case of the integrating developing countries, trade has helped improve labour standards and trade sanctions are most likely to have the opposite effect. It is important to realize that low labour standards in developing countries generally reflect deep-seated problems of unemployment, underemployment and poverty, rather than unwillingness of governments to improve labour standards. It is through a process of overcoming the problems of unemployment, underemployment and poverty that labour standards can be improved; and there is no instant "one size fits all" solution to these problems. All this means that the ILO's well-established approach to improving labour standards – through consultations and technical assistance – remains valid in the era of globalization. The approach makes it possible to view the problem of improving labour standards as a part of the problem of overcoming unemployment, underemployment and poverty, and allows for country-specific strategies. However, strengthening the organization's mandate and capacity to conduct *ex ante* assessments of the possible labour market effects of trade agreements and liberalization programmes could enhance the effectiveness of the ILO's approach. Such a strengthening is an objective that the international community could fruitfully pursue.

REFERENCES

Acemoglu, D. 2002. "Technical change, inequality and the labour market", in *Journal of Economic Literature*, Vol. 40, No. 1, pp. 7–72.

Arndt, S.W.; Kierzkowski, H. (eds.). 2001. *Fragmentation: New production patterns in the world economy* (Oxford, Oxford University Press).

Bairoch, P.; Kozul-Wright, R. 1998. "Globalization myths: Some historical reflections on integration, industrialization and growth in the world economy", in Kozul-Wright and Rowthorn (eds.), 1998.

Behrman, J.R.; Birdsall, N.; Székely, M. 2000. *Economic reform and wage differentials in Latin America*, Working Paper No. 435 (Washington, DC, Inter-American Development Bank).

Berry, A.; Bourguignon, F.; Morrisson, C. 1983. "Changes in the world distribution of income between 1950 and 1977", in *Economic Journal*, Vol. 93, No. 370, pp. 331–350.

Bhagwati, J. 2002. *Free trade today* (Princeton and Oxford, Princeton University Press).

Birdsall, N. 1988. "Economic approaches to population growth and development", in H.B. Chenery and T.N. Srinivasan (eds.): *Handbook of Development Economics* (Amsterdam, North-Holland).

Borjas, G.J. 1994. "The economics of immigration", in *Journal of Economic Literature*, Vol. 32, No. 4, pp. 1667–1717.

—. 1995. "The economic benefits from immigration", in *Journal of Economic Perspectives*, Vol. 9, pp. 3–22.

—; Freeman, R.B. (eds.). 1992. *Immigration and the workforce: Economic consequences for the United States and source areas* (Chicago, Chicago University Press).

Bourguignon, F.; Morrisson, C. 2002. "Inequality among world citizens: 1820–1992", in *American Economic Review*, Vol. 92, No. 4, pp. 727–744.

—; Coyle, D.; Fernandez, R.; Giavazzi, F.; Martin, D.; O'Rourke, K.; Portes, R.; Seabright, P.; Vennables, A.; Verdier, T.; Winters, L.A.. 2002. *Making sense of globalization: A guide to the economic issues*, Policy Paper No. 8 (London, Centre for Economic Policy Research).

Brown, D.K. 2001. "Labour standards: Where do they belong on the international trade agenda?", in *Journal of Economic Perspectives*, Vol. 15, No. 3, pp. 89–112.

Campa, J.; Goldberg, L. 1997. "The evolving external orientation of manufacturing industries", in *Economic Policy Review* (Federal Reserve Bank of New York), Vol. 3, No. 2, pp. 53–81.Chen, S.; Wang, Y. 2001. *China's growth and poverty reduction: Trends between 1990 and 1999*, Working Paper No. 2651 (Washington, DC, World Bank).

—; Ravallion, M. 2001. *How did the world's poorest fare in the 1990s?* Development Research Group, World Bank (Washington, DC, World Bank; processed).

Cline, W.R. 1997. *Trade, jobs and income distribution* (Washington, DC, Institute for International Economics).

Collier, P.; Gunning, J.W. 1999. "Explaining African economic performance", in *Journal of Economic Literature*, Vol. 37, No. 1, pp. 64–111.

Collins, S. (ed.). 1998. *Exports, imports and the American worker* (Washington, DC, Brookings Institution Press).

Crafts, N. 2000. *Globalization and growth in the twentieth century*, Working Paper WP/00/44 (Washington, DC, IMF).

Datt, G.; Ravallion, M. 2002. *Is India's economic growth leaving the poor behind?*, Working Paper No. 2846 (Washington, DC, World Bank).

Deininger, K.; Squire, L. 1996. "A new data set measuring income inequality", in *The World Bank Economic Review*, Vol. 10, No. 3, pp. 565–591.

Devan, J.; Tewari, P.S. 2001. "Brains abroad", in *McKinsey Quarterly*, No. 4, pp. 51–60.

Dewatripont, M.; Sapir, A.; Sekkat, K. 1999. *Trade and jobs in Europe: Much ado about nothing?* (Oxford, Oxford University Press).

ECLA [United Nations Economic Commission for Latin America]. 1950. *The economic development of Latin America and its principal problems* (New York).

ECLAC [United Nations Economic Commission for Latin America and the Caribbean]. 2002. *Globalization and development* (Santiago).

Faini, R., de Mello, J.; Zimmermann, K.F. (eds.). 1999. *Migration: The controversies and the evidence* (Cambridge, Cambridge University Press).

Feenstra, R.C. 1998. "Integration of trade and disintegration of production", in *Journal of Economic Perspectives*, Vol. 12, No. 4, pp. 31–50.

—; Hanson, G.H. 1996. "Foreign investment, outsourcing and relative wages", in R.C. Feenstra et al. (eds.): *The political economy of trade policy: Essays in honor of Jagdish Bhagwati* (Cambrige, MA, MIT Press), pp. 89–128.

—; —. 1997. "Foreign direct investment and relative wages: Evidence from Mexico's maquiladoras", *Journal of International Economics*, Vol. 42, Nos. 3/4, pp. 371–394.

—; —. 2001. *Global production sharing and rising inequality: A survey of trade and wages*, Working Paper No. 8372 (Cambridge, MA, National Bureau of Economic Research).

Ferriera, F.H.G.; Paes de Barros, R. 1999. *The slippery slope: Explaining the increase in extreme poverty in urban Brazil, 1976–1996*, Working Paper No. 2210 (Washington, DC, World Bank).

Freeman, R.B. 1994. "A hard-headed look at labour standards", in W. Sengenberger and D. Campbell (eds.): *International labour standards and economic interdependence* (Geneva, ILO).

Ghose, A.K. 2000. *Trade liberalization and manufacturing employment*, Employment Paper 2000/3 (Geneva, ILO).

—. 2001. *Global economic inequality and international trade*, Employment Paper 2001/12 (Geneva, ILO).

—. 2002. *Trade and international labour mobility*, Employment Paper 2002/33 (Geneva, ILO).

—. Forthcoming. "Global inequality and international trade", forthcoming in *Cambridge Journal of Economics*.

—; Matsumoto, M. 2002. *Trade and the restructuring of international division of labour* (Geneva, ILO; draft paper).

Goldar, B.N. 2002. *Trade liberalization and manufacturing employment: The case of India*, Employment Paper 2002/34 (Geneva, ILO).

Golub, S.S. 1999. *Labour costs and international trade* (Washington, DC, The AEI Press).

Harrisson, A.; Hanson, G. 1999. "Who gains from trade reform? Some remaining puzzles", in *Journal of Development Economics*, Vol. 59, No. 1, pp. 125–154.

Howell, J.; Kambhampati, U. 1999. "Liberalization and labour: The fate of retrenched workers in the cotton textile industry in India", in *Oxford Development Studies*, Vol. 27, No. 1, pp. 109–128.

Hufbauer, G.C.; Berliner, D.T.; Elliot, K.A. 1986. *Trade protection in the United States: 31 case studies* (Washington, DC, Institute for International Economics).

Hummels, D., Ishii, J.; Yi, K.M. 2001. "The nature and growth of vertical specialization in world trade", in *Journal of International Economics*, Vol. 54, No. 1, pp. 75–96.

ILO [International Labour Organization]. 1998. *Labour and social issues relating to export processing zones* (Geneva).

IMF [International Monetary Fund]. 2001. *World Economic Outlook*, October (Washington, DC).

Irwin, D.A. 2002. *Free trade under fire* (Princeton and Oxford, Princeton University Press).

Jasso, G.; Rosenzweig, M.; Smith, J. 1998. *The changing skill of new immigrants to the United States: Recent trends and their determinants*, Working Paper 6764 (Cambridge, MA, National Bureau of Economic Research).

Kelley, A.C. 1988. "Economic consequences of population change in the Third World", in *Journal of Economic Literature*, Vol. 26, No. 4, pp. 1685–1728.

Keynes, J.M. 1973. *The general theory of employment, interest and money*, The Royal Economic Society edition (Cambridge, Cambridge University Press).

Kozul-Wright, R.; Rowthorn, R. (eds.). 1998. *Transnational corporations and the global economy* (Helsinki, WIDER).

Krugman, P. 1995. "Growing world trade: Causes and consequences", in *Brookings Papers on Economic Activity*, Vol. 1, pp. 327–377.

—. 2000. "Technology, trade and factor prices", in *Journal of International Economics*, Vol. 50, No. 1, pp. 51–71.

Kucera, D. 2001. *The effects of core workers' rights on labour cost and FDI: Evaluating the conventional wisdom*, International Institute for Labour Studies Discussion Paper DP/130/2001 (Geneva, ILO).

——; Milberg, W. 2002. *Trade and the loss of manufacturing jobs in the OECD: New factor content calculations for 1978–1995*, International Institute for Labour Studies Discussion Paper DP/135/2002 (Geneva, ILO).

Lall, S. 2001. "The technological structure and performance of developing country manufactured exports, 1985–98", in *Oxford Development Studies*, Vol. 28, No. 3, pp. 337–369.

Landesmann, M.; Stehrer, R.; Leitner, S. 2002. *Trade liberalization and labour markets: Perspective from OECD economies*, Employment Paper 2002/41 (Geneva, ILO).

Lee, D.S. 1999. "Wage inequality in the United States during the 1980s: Rising dispersion or falling minimum wage?", in *Quarterly Journal of Economics*, Vol. 114, No. 3, pp. 977–1023.

Lee, E. 1997. "Globalization and labour standards: A review of issues", in *International Labour Review*, Vol. 136, No. 2, pp. 173–189.

——. 1998. *The Asian financial crisis: The challenge for social policy* (Geneva, ILO).

Li, H.; Squire, L.; Zou, H.F. 1998. "Explaining international and intertemporal variations in income inequality", in *Economic Journal*, Vol. 108, No. 446, pp. 26–43.

Maskus, K. 1997. "Should core labour standards be imposed through international trade policy?", Policy Research Working Paper No. 1817 (Washington, DC, World Bank).

Milanovic, B. 2000. "True world inequality 1988 and 1993: First calculations based on household surveys alone", Policy Research Working Paper No. 2244 (Washington, DC, World Bank).

——. 2002. "The two faces of globalization: Against globalization as we know it", (Washington, DC, World Bank; processed).

Milner, H.V. 1988. *Resisting protectionism: Global industries and the politics of international trade* (Princeton, Princeton University Press).

Moran, T.H. 2002. *Beyond sweatshops: Foreign direct investment and globalization in developing countries* (Washington, DC, Brookings Institution Press).

Nayyar, D. 2000. *Cross-border movements of people*, Working Paper No. 194 (Helsinki, WIDER).

OECD [Organisation for Economic Co-operation and Development]. 1983. *Industrial adjustment and government support* (Paris).

——. 1994. *The OECD Jobs Study: Evidence and Explanation* (Paris).

——. 1996. *Trade, employment and labour standards: A study of core workers' rights and international trade* (Paris).

——. 2000. *International trade and core labour standards* (Paris).

——. 2001. *Employment Outlook, 2001* (Paris).

O'Rourke, K.H.; Williamson, J.G. 1999. *Globalization and history: The evolution of a nineteenth century Atlantic economy* (Cambridge, MA, MIT Press).

Oxfam. 2002. *Rigged rules and double standards: Trade, globalisation, and the fight against poverty* (London).

Palma, G. 2002. *The labour market effects of trade liberalization in Mexico* (Geneva, ILO; draft paper).

Prebisch, R. 1959. "Commercial policies in underdeveloped countries", in *American Economic Review*, Vol. 49, No. 2, pp. 251–273.

Rasiah, R. 2002. *Manufactured exports, employment, skills and wages in Malaysia*, Employment Paper 2002/35 (Geneva, ILO).

Revenga, A. 1995. *Employment and wage effects of trade liberalization: The case of Mexican manufacturing*, Policy Research Working Paper 1524 (Washington, DC, World Bank).

Rodrik, D. 1997. *Has globalization gone too far?* (Washington, DC, Institute for International Economics).

—. 1999. "Democracies pay higher wages", in *Quarterly Journal of Economics*, Vol. 114, No. 3, pp. 707–738.

Rowthorn, R.; Ramaswamy, R. 1997. *Growth, trade and deindustrialization*, Working Paper WP/97/42 (Washington, DC, IMF).

Sachs, J.; Warner, A. 1995. "Economic reform and the process of global integration", in *Brookings Papers on Economic Activity*, Vol. 1, pp. 1–118.

Sala-i-Martin, X. 2002. *The world distribution of income (estimated from individual country distributions)*, Department of Economics Discussion Paper No. 0102–58 (New York, Columbia University).

Schultz, T.P. 1998. "Inequality in the distribution of personal income in the world: How it is changing and why", in *Journal of Population Economics*, Vol. 11, No. 2, pp. 307–344.

Singer, H. 1950. "The distribution of gains between investing and borrowing countries", in *American Economic Review*, Vol. 40, No. 2, pp. 473–485.

Singh, A.; Zammit, A. 2000. *The global labour standards controversy: Critical issues for developing countries* (Geneva, South Centre).

Slaughter, M.J. 1998. "International trade and labour market outcomes: Results, questions, and policy options", in *Economic Journal*, Vol. 108, No. 450, pp. 1452–1462.

—. 2000. *Protectionist tendencies in the North and vulnerable economies in the South*, Working Paper No. 196 (Helsinki, WIDER).

Solimano, A. 2001. *International migration and the global economic order: An overview*, Policy Research Working Paper No. 2720 (Washington, DC, World Bank).

Stiglitz, J.E. 2002. *Globalization and its discontents* (New York and London, W.W. Norton & Company).

Tharakan, P.K.M. 2000. *The problem of anti-dumping protection and developing country exports*, Working Paper No. 198 (Helsinki, WIDER).

UNCTAD [United Nations Conference on Trade and Development]. 1998. *Trade and Development Report 1998* (Geneva and New York).

—. 2000. *World Investment Report 2000* (Geneva and New York).

—. 2002. *Trade and Development Report 2002* (Geneva and New York).

—. 2002a. *The Least Developed Countries Report 2002: Escaping the Poverty Trap* (Geneva and New York).

UNDP [United Nations Development Programme]. 1999. *Human Development Report 1999* (New York and Oxford, Oxford University Press).

United Nations, Population Division, Department of Economic and Social Affairs. 2000. *Replacement migration: Is it a solution to declining and ageing populations?* (New York).

Vernengo, M. 2002. *External liberalization, macroeconomic instability and the labour market in Brazil* (Geneva, ILO; draft paper).

Wilkins, M. 1998. "Multinational corporations: An historical account", in Kozul-Wright and Rowthorn (eds.), 1998.

Woo, W.T.; Ren, R. 2002. *Employment, wages and income inequality in the internationalization of China's economy* (Geneva, ILO; draft paper).

Wood, A. 1994. *North–South trade, employment and inequality* (Oxford, Clarendon Press).

—. 1995. "How trade hurt unskilled workers", in *Journal of Economic Perspectives*, Vol. 9, No. 3, pp. 57–80.

—. 1997. "Openness and wage inequality in developing countries: The Latin American challenge to East Asian conventional wisdom", in *World Bank Economic Review*, Vol. 11, No. 1, pp. 33–57.

—. 1998. "Globalization and the rise of labour market inequalities", *Economic Journal*, Vol. 108, No. 450, pp. 1463–1482.

World Bank. 2001. *Globalization, growth and poverty: Building an inclusive world economy* (Washington, DC, World Bank, and Oxford, Oxford University Press).

—. 2002. *Global economic prospects and developing countries* (Washington, DC).

Yeats, A. 2001. "Just how big is global production sharing?", in Arndt and Kierzkowski (eds.), 2001.

Zimmermann, K.F. 1995. "Tackling the European migration problem", in *Journal of Economic Perspectives*, Vol. 9, No. 2, pp. 45–62.

INDEX

Note:Page numbers in **bold** refer to tables, those in *italic* to figures; *n* appended to a page number indicates a footnote.

DATE DUE
